CW00976695

Dear Liz (Lily)

Connected!

Stay

2014

connected

To my family and Mother Nature, who continue to inspire me.

connected

the sustainable landscapes of
PHILLIP JOHNSON

MURDOCH BOOKS

Foreword

To marvel at Mother Nature is to be in awe of her snowy mountains, rainforests, raging rivers, endless seas, rocky deserts and sandy beaches. To be fascinated by the sweep of wonders on the wing, and creeping crawling insects; to be hooked by the wildlife—big and small; to walk blinded by the colours, and be struck dumb by the sounds of winds, waves and weather. To be captured by the perfumes of the evening, warmed by sunsoaked stones and chilled by twilight dew.

Our landscapes are extraordinary. Our souls are at their mercy. Our wellbeing tied to their very presence. Just a glimpse, just a glance, can change our moods. There can be few more compelling instincts than the urge to embrace a beautiful view. It's simply irresistible. The shiny falling apple which is the gravity of place. All of us, young or old, are drawn by a fundamental lure of the land, as natural as a Cootamundra bloom.

But just as seeing a beautiful landscape can take the breath away, being immersed in one can be a life-changing encounter. To touch it, to spend time in it, to share it with loved ones, to be moved by it, to let it gently elevate our spirits. The great outdoors remains life's great canvas.

This is the world of Phillip Johnson. Nature doing what nature does best.

Our living landscapes are Phillip's palette. And what an artist he is. The seemingly bottomless pit of passion and energy that is Phillip will engage you, inspire you, charm you and captivate you.

Phillip's gardens are for gazing at and from—but most of all for experiencing and sharing. And you can be sure you'll give yourself to a Phillip Johnson garden in ways you may never have imagined.

When Phillip with his partners, Wes Fleming and Dylan Brady and their team, combined their talents to scoop the pool at the 2013 Centenary Chelsea Flower Show in London, they achieved what no other Australians had done before—'Best in Show'! They danced about in delight, hugging each other and wiping away tears of joy. On the other side of the world we did too.

The story of their Chelsea triumph is an epic. It is a story made for goose bumps and lumpy throats. Years of planning and dedication were essential. But Phillip's design to transform a flat stretch of urban park in London into an intimate, multi-levelled, multi-layered slice of the Australian landscape was an inspiration. So detailed was the design that Her Majesty when visiting asked Phillip (not *her* Philip!) about the frogs in the garden—in fact, what our beaming Queen had heard was Phillip's pre-recorded frog sounds placed sweetly and discreetly in the garden. This is where Phillip excels—transforming outdoor spaces into places of love and other muses.

Every garden has its reason. But each is of and from nature. Water circling in play with the clarity of rain. Plants selected for their very essence. Rocks and logs placed as if they had always been there. Each garden in context but each a place where all seems as one.

The detail in Phillip's landscapes and gardens is exquisite. It is beautifully balanced to sustain itself. And to build a much bigger whole that is a living piece of our natural heritage.

Phillip's home state is Victoria. Our Indigenous heritage combines with the achievements of the free settlers who came from all corners of the world, largely from the 1850s onwards, with a firm eye on the future.

The civic legacy they have left us is remarkable: our parliamentary precinct, town halls, court houses, churches and stately homes. It is at the core of our state's identity, as is Victoria's worldwide reputation for magnificent gardens. Victoria will always be Australia's Garden State.

The energetic, youthful and multicultural spirit of our forebears is with us all every day. There is nothing that can't be done here if we put our minds to the task. Phillip has that spirit in abundance. And it shows. It's fresh and brave and intoxicating.

I met Phillip many years ago at the wonderful International Flower and Garden Show in Melbourne's World Heritage-listed Exhibition Buildings set in the beautiful Carlton Gardens. He was accepting, with typical pent-up emotion, a well-earned award. Some years later, as Premier of Victoria, I had the pleasure of ensuring that Phillip's team had the backing they needed for their mission at Chelsea. Their win, their excitement, was something we could all share. The creative talent in our state was again being appreciated across the world. In Phillip's work you may not find what you expect or what you've found before. You won't find topiary. You won't find trimmed hedges. Or giant pots. Or lawns to showcase a budding creative mower. You won't find obedient roses and camellias all in a row. And you won't find cast-iron gazebos or paved paths. But you will know truly beautiful gardens. You'll experience the transformations. And you will find places where children and birds choose to be and choose to explore.

Could we want for more? And what a continuing legacy that is for all Australians.

Phillip Johnson does magic—in the garden!

Ted Baillieu
Premier of Victoria
2010–2013

Contents

Introduction

I grew up in Glen Waverley, Victoria, in the heart of suburbia. My dad loved working outdoors, and from a very young age I used to work alongside him. I just wanted to be outside, helping him potter in the garden. My gran and pa on my father's side lived in a California bungalow in Caulfield South. The front of the garden was very traditionally English, with hydrangeas and birches, and they also had a beautiful jacaranda tree. Every time I visited, I would walk up the western side of the garden through a fernery. The paths were made of crushed-up shell grit my gran collected from the beach, and I still recall the texture and the sound of walking on that shell surface. It was so tactile, and it crunched under our feet. There was a little area where we could dig. I could move rocks around and make little ponds and creeks. The exterior of my pa's shed was covered in electric-blue morning glory, and we used to go in and see all his tools hanging up. My pa never threw anything out. I learnt about re-using and being self-sufficient from him. I learnt that *everything* can be used!

My grandparents' house had a produce garden out the back, which supplied them with lemons, blood plums, pears, apricots and apples. There were no sprays, so everything was organic. We also had our little area within the veggie patch where I could dig with my brothers. That's how I learnt about growing potatoes and carrots. This is where I now see the future—that every garden we design has some form of fruit, vegetables or herbs growing in it, even if it's just a pot of basil.

My great-grandfather had a goldmine in Reedy Creek, Victoria. He always used to tell me tales about goldmining, rocks and tunnels, and I used to love hearing that story of stone, and dreaming about it. That's part of the reason I love rock.

Both my sets of grandparents were quite exceptional horticulturalists. My grandparents on my mother's side had a very manicured, traditional church garden. My Papa Vic was very creative with timber and design, and good at building things. Out the back they also had a fabulous produce garden. Nanna always had bags of tomatoes, and silverbeet and beans that supplied the family with fresh veggies.

I have two older brothers. As a child I loved being outside and getting dirty. I used to get really excited whenever there was a storm. I would just hang out beside the road when it was raining and watch the enormous amount of water that flowed off the road into the gutters. That's how I discovered where it all went.

When I was about eight, my parents recognised my love of gardening and gave me a 2 metre by 2 metre space in their backyard to design and build in. I was able to shape and sculpt my own garden using materials from their property, including bluestone pitchers and rocks.

I attended Caulfield Grammar School and, academically, I found things very difficult. I was diagnosed as being extremely dyslexic. For years I had one-on-one teaching, helping me behind the scenes to learn to read and write. I struggled so much at school—and it's a good

---

Opposite
Clockwise from top left: *Scaevola aemula* 'Mauve Clusters'; *Grevillea* 'Bonfire'; *Brachyscome multifida*; *Dianella longifolia*; *Anigozanthos flavidus* 'Big Red'; Me fishing with my gran; *Actinotus helianthi* (flannel flowers); Me as a child, sitting in a field of daffodils.
Centre: *Xerochrysum bracteatum* (everlasting daisies).

Introduction

thing for young people to know that. You can get through anything, but you've got to believe in yourself. Find out what gives you that special buzz and then go for it. For me, it was horticulture.

As a child I also found it very difficult to distinguish between reds, greens and browns, and blues and purples. Hundreds of times over the years, when people have found out I'm colour-blind, they've asked: 'How on earth can you design a garden?'

So how do I make it work? My dad is an incredible art educator. He's taught me the importance of the colour wheel. As an example, for our planting design at the Chelsea Flower Show, I knew we wanted warm to hot colours—such as reds, oranges and yellows—in the foreground, and cooler, recessive colours—such as blues, purples, pinks and whites—at the top of the gorge, which allowed us to create a depth of colour within our range.

My dad is a landscape painter. The fascination for a lot of artists is light and atmosphere and natural surfaces. He taught me to view the world in a creative way. When I design something, I still describe it as evolving like a landscape painting. You're painting it within the earth, but it actually comes alive.

When I was sixteen, I discovered rock climbing. That was when my whole world changed. I climbed everywhere. I used to climb on the walls of the Glen Waverley library and other buildings. I became a climbing instructor and started taking people up as a student guide. During the Christmas holidays one year, I caught a train to Arapiles, past Horsham in Victoria. Arapiles is an amazing sandstone cliff. It's regarded as one of the best spots to climb in the world. From then on, I was climbing there almost every holiday and long weekend. As I matured, it wasn't just about the climb anymore—I also fell in love with the nearby Grampians National Park. By then I had started to love the whole experience: the walk, the environment, the seasonal changes, the calls of the birds, the smells, the secluded waterholes and the waterfalls.

On these trips I used to pass dry creekbeds and noticed that sometimes they were filled with water. So I started to observe the fluctuation of water levels in nature. And I loved the beautiful rocks around the edge of the waterholes.

When it came time to apply for university, I made a mistake on my application form and accidentally got into primary teaching instead of horticulture! So I deferred for a year, to do a traineeship in outdoor education at Caulfield Grammar School's Yarra Junction campus. That was one of the best years of my life. I lived down at Wilsons Promontory National Park for a few months, which is home to massive boulders, spectacular vegetation and some of the most beautiful beaches in the world. It was inspirational to be surrounded by this beautiful environment, to see how the rock connected with the land and water. That's where I first observed how children really enjoy themselves when they are surrounded by nature. That's when I started to realise, 'I could build this for myself. I could create these environments for people to live in.'

I then got into a horticulture degree at Burnley, at the University of Melbourne, which at the time was the best horticulture course in Australia. We had to learn the botanical names of thousands of plants. I taught myself a lot of the names just by studying and hand-drawing the specimens.

———————

Opposite
A view of the lower wetland at Lubra Bend.

Once I graduated, I started my business. After I'd built my mum and dad's garden, I created a garden in East Ringwood, which was the first time I collected water to sustain a billabong. This was one of the first projects where we were harnessing water run-off and directing it into a little frog bog. We used solar energy to power a small pump. This garden was the first step in the direction I wanted to take things.

I wanted to start replicating the environments found in nature, which included creating waterfalls. I also wanted to build my own company that would create its own energy and make a big difference to this planet.

I was fortunate to be able to travel during this time. I jumped at every opportunity. After working at Frost Valley YMCA in the state of New York, USA, I travelled throughout South America. Among the highlights for me were Iguazu Falls on the border of Argentina and Brazil—the second largest waterfall in the world—and Machu Picchu in Peru. I also travelled throughout Chile, from the extreme beauty of the Atacama Desert through to the amazing remnant forests of *Araucaria araucana*, also known as the monkey puzzle tree.

But what I have always loved is Japanese design. I travelled around Japan and saw how the Japanese work with rock and water. These are landscapes that have lasted for hundreds of years and the results are tranquil oases that revive the soul and nurture the environment. My favourite Japanese garden is the Moss Garden of Saiho-ji, just outside Kyoto. It's over 675 years old. I see it as my benchmark: I want all my landscapes to stand the test of time, like this one, and last hundreds of years and many generations.

In 2000, our company built a landscape at Kinvarra, a massive property in Wandin North, Victoria. It was the first large landscape that I had built, and we entered it in the landscape industry awards. It won the Water Wise Award, and also took out the Landscape of the Year Award. That was the big turning point for the company. Working on Kinvarra gave me the confidence to tackle other big projects. We undertook a dam conversion in Wonga Park, Victoria, converting a traditional dam in an established landscape so that it would be sustained using collected water from the property. A whole range of different species of frogs, birds, butterflies and bees are thriving there now.

Something I always talk about is my 80/20 principle. At the moment, most Australian urban landscapes are made up of 80 per cent hard surfaces and only 20 per cent permeable surfaces. My aim is to switch those numbers around.

Landscape design trends over the last twenty years have drawn some of their inspiration from English landscapes, which we know after going through many droughts aren't suitable for all locations. We've seen garden designs featuring only a few species, but this is really just supporting a monoculture. We've seen the introduction of synthetic turf. We've seen the incorporation of outdoor kitchen and lifestyle entertaining spaces. But such designs are often lacking in soul and beauty. Sustainable principles should drive the landscape design brief. Don't get me wrong, entertaining spaces are vital. But we can incorporate them as a secondary element, with the primary element being gardens that nourish and heal us. After we won Best in Show at Chelsea in 2013, the judges said how beautiful it was to see a garden with such soul again, not just another take on an outdoor kitchen.

———

Opposite
Top: Large stepping stones allow for access across the billabong at Wonga Park.

Bottom: The jetty at Wonga Park was built from reclaimed iron bark and provides a great fishing or dining platform.

We need to create healing habitats to make things better again; to repair what we've done to the environment. And this can be achieved one garden at a time. It can start in your own backyard.

Water is tranquil and soothing. It has its own mood at different times of the day—the light catches it and turns it different colours—and it supports an amazing diversity of aquatic life. That's why it's the soul of our designs.

For the future of this planet, to be smart in urban design we need to capture our water and retain it within our homes and communities. As you'll see in this book, we have many examples of clients living in rural and urban environments who are using minimal mains water.

In this day and age we are becoming more and more detached from nature. We've forgotten how healing it is to be surrounded by beauty. Connecting with the earth is one of the most invigorating and energising things you can do. Whether you are just getting your hands dirty, plucking out a weed, planting herbs, swimming in your natural pool, or simply sitting surrounded by nature as you read the weekend paper—gardens slow you down. They de-stress you. They heal you. This is why it's so important for people to create beautiful environments for themselves and their families.

In *Connected*, you'll find examples of landscapes that range from large rural properties to some of the smallest spaces you can garden in, but the element that connects them is how people's lives have been transformed, and how, in turn, our living environment and this planet can be rejuvenated. If there's one thing I want people to get from this book, it's that this vision can be achieved anywhere, from farms to suburban blocks to rooftops.

My garden, that's where I go to re-energise. There's so much going on. The fish, the ripples on the billabong, the friendly robins drinking the water, the kookaburras diving, the wallabies chewing on the kangaroo paw flowers. We're healing the environment by bringing back nature, and we're healing ourselves at the same time. In the end, it's all about natural beauty. Beauty heals the soul. And what I want to do is surround everyone with it.

Opposite
The billabong from the Rock Garden.

Introduction

An English Garden

An English Garden

This is my parents' home, where I grew up, and their garden has always been my playground. My father always encouraged me and my brothers to help him around the garden, and one of my earliest memories is of helping him train and prune the ornamental grapevine and collecting all the cuttings. As a kid, this was where I would build little gardens and just watch things grow; it was a place where I could play with pets, prune plants and grow vegetables. Later on it was my playground in a different sense.

In my final year of university, I had the privilege of redesigning and rebuilding my parents' front garden. It's quite English and formal, which is how they wanted it. As you can see, this landscape is significantly different from what I do now. My parents love English garden plants, and it's interesting that the journey I've been on is the exact opposite of that! I'm passionate about our beautiful Australian species, and I see the need for working more with our indigenous vegetation. But while my forte is designing with Australian native plants, I'm able to work in a lot of different styles. One of the most important things my team and I take into account when developing a project is respecting the owners' needs and wishes, and it was the same back at the beginning of my career.

I think the way my parents use plants is exceptional: from softening the front fence with the ficus climber, to meticulously pruning and training the ornamental grapevine to create a lovely plant wall that helps cool the verandah. It's one of my favourite parts of this garden. We've had many a Christmas lunch with the whole family out here, sometimes up to thirty people. The ornamental grapevine cools the environment beautifully and creates a natural canopy, but it also allows a beautiful rich light into the space in winter. When the sun comes through in the morning, you get a glowing diffused flood of green. This is a great design feature, and I use it in many projects.

The plant selection is really driven by my father, and many of them came from his parents—plants can be passed down through generations. The clivias were originally growing in a pot, and they've now been divided and planted throughout the whole property. Clivias are a very water-efficient plant, and they're great to have under a tree because they're so resilient.

My parents also received some hydrangea cuttings from my grandparents' garden. My dad planted the hydrangeas where they're protected from the late-afternoon sun. He uses them as inspiration for his still-life drawings. It always fascinated me how the flower colour responded to the pH level of the soil, and led me to wonder how I could apply this science to the bodies of water my team and I created in our projects. So at the 2012 Melbourne International Flower and Garden Show I used a hydrangea planted on the edge of the billabong to highlight the pH levels of the water.

Most of the plants in the fernery have come from my great-aunt, and they're all quite rare and unusual. Many of them are seventy years old, and we share them around the family. When my great-grandparents came to Australia from England, they brought one pot of aspidistra with them, and all the aspidistra

Previous pages
The viewing window into the secret garden beyond the wall. *Ficus pumila* covers the garden wall, with *Stachys byzantina* as a border.

Opposite
Hydrangea spp.

plants in the fernery are grown from that one pot. This plant collection could be described as a family album; each plant is a bit like the family brooch that's handed down through generations.

The aspidistra is beautiful. It's a typical English plant and it's also referred to as the cast-iron plant because, no matter what, it doesn't die. One aspect that I've challenged my father on (and he's got his own opinions), are the environmental weeds, such as ivy, within their garden. It used to be everywhere, over every fence, but he's been very good at reducing it in recent years. Ivy is a highly invasive weed—it can take over whole tree canopies, and it sucks out moisture from buildings, so it's not something I recommend to people. A similar climber is Virginia creeper, which is not as invasive and has beautiful autumn foliage. Another option is a ficus climber. In Australia, we don't have native climbers that attach to walls.

My parents also used to have container plants that needed constant irrigation. I encouraged my father to grow really water-efficient plants, such as succulents, in the pots instead, to reduce the need for watering.

What's also great about this place is that it's surrounded by trees, which help cool the house during the summer months, and warm it in winter. Because the trees are all deciduous, the sun can come through in the cooler months.

The front gravel area was originally lawn, and when I was growing up the garden featured rounded garden beds. In redesigning the space we've retained the existing birches and created a sandstone formal entertaining space for long lunches out there. When it used to be just a lawn there was no functional surface to entertain on. Lawn is suitable in certain applications, but it's very high-maintenance: you need to water it to sustain it, along with adding fertilisers and chemicals to it. You have to design the right solution for each property. In this garden we're surrounded by a beautiful landscape—it's not all hard-surface entertaining area. My whole design drive is to create soul and energy in an outdoor space. Things like outdoor barbecues shouldn't be the design drivers, the landscape should be. Lots of hard surfaces mean the area is non-permeable when it rains, which can cause problems with flooding.

Something that in hindsight I would have done very differently is the way I drained the sandstone entertaining area towards the house. If I did it again, I would drain the water away from the house, into the garden, where it can naturally irrigate the soil profile. And this is why it's great to trial things. Planning is pivotal when you design a landscape, and so is getting all your levels and level changes correct. So that's something I've learnt from this build: where possible, always drain away from the house.

My parents respect that my approach is different from theirs. They try to be receptive to my advice. We've all taught each other over the years. They've been open to some things, but not everything ... They still don't have a billabong in their front yard! I guess you could call what they have a 'formal billabong'. I created a very angular, very formal L-shaped pond. It was a great project because I'd never built a pond before, and it was very challenging. There are water lilies and water snails and around thirty fish in there, which my parents never have to feed.

Opposite
Clockwise from top left:
Hydrangea spp., *Pontederia cordata*, *Salvia leucantha*, *Alstroemeria* cultivar.

With every project my team and I try to incorporate some body of water, because it just creates so much energy and diversity within the landscape. I often talk about the soul of the landscape being the billabong. One of my inspirations for creating ponds and water features was my next-door neighbour, who would build a frog pond in all the properties he lived in and in this way add his signature.

What is great about my parents' pond is that it fluctuates according to the rainfall. They don't fill it up with mains water, so they are actually applying the same principles as I apply to my billabongs. It's fairly low-maintenance as well. This means simply cutting back water lilies and irises in the wintertime, and removing the organic matter.

When my parents built their house they wanted to install a rainwater tank, but at the time (forty-odd years ago) the council wouldn't give them permission. It sounds ludicrous now. As a result, one of the biggest challenges here is irrigation, because the garden does require a lot of water. This is where my drive for promoting the importance of collecting water started.

Growing up, I can remember significant times throughout my childhood where we had severe water restrictions. And it was just fascinating to see how my parents conserved water during those times—using grey water from the bath, shower and kitchen to help sustain the garden. But after the restrictions were lifted I saw them going back to their old habits of using mains water for irrigation and watering the garden morning and night. And I wondered: do you really need to water as much as you think you do? This has really influenced my design approach: how to design a landscape that needs next to no irrigation. I encourage people to install rainwater tanks so this water can be used to irrigate the garden.

At Burnley College I learnt all about the water requirements of certain plants, and I thought there was a lot of room for improvement. In Australia, water needs to be seen as the most precious resource we have.

I now design landscapes where watering only occurs during the establishment phase. If there's any water to be used, if watering is required, we've zoned the garden accordingly—for example, to reflect the fact that vegetables require frequent watering. I'm now noticing a shift in attitude—it's often compulsory to install a rainwater tank. They might take up a bit of space but it is worth it. I try to encourage everyone to be as self-sufficient as possible.

My sons are starting to play in my parents' garden in the same way I used to. Now they go to their grandparents' home and have these wonderful experiences too … Exploring in the backyard, playing with water, searching for fairies and sitting in shaded corners having little chats.

I loved what I created here, but it was really the turning point with my design approach. From then on, I wanted to create something different. This garden was influenced a lot by the design trend at the time, which was formal English landscapes. There isn't a single Australian native plant in it. This fact drove and inspired me to think differently.

Above: A traditional English-style planting, which includes species such as *Salvia leucantha, Rosmarinus officinalis* and *Pontederia cordata*.

Left: *Stachys byzantina*, also known as lamb's ear, is a hardy perennial known for its thick woolly leaves. It works well when filling an area of your landscape and as a border.

Opposite
Hedera helix (common ivy) has been declared an environmental weed in Victoria. However, my father keeps it under control by limiting it to a few locations in the garden.

The fernery range of
shade-loving plants.

Opposite
Top: *Vitis vinifera* growing over
the pergola provides cool relief.

Bottom: *Pontederia cordata* was
planted in the formal pond.

Following pages
The colourful flowers in this
English garden include an
Alstroemeria cultivar, *Strelitzia
reginae* and *Hydrangea* spp.

My Home

My Home

Olinda, my own property in the Dandenong Ranges, forty minutes from Melbourne, is set on 7 acres (2.8 hectares), with filtered views out to the Yarra Valley. We're surrounded by this beautiful natural amphitheatre of mountain ash (*Eucalyptus regnans*), which is the tallest flowering plant in the world. The energy that these trees give the landscape is of great magnitude. We have such a wonderful borrowed landscape to work with.

In my line of work, everything—techniques, materials, approaches and more—is continually evolving. You get better and better as you discover new ways of doing things. I'm lucky to be able to test out all my ideas at Olinda. I use it as a place where I can try new things and show people what's possible.

After finishing my degree at Burnley, and before I bought Olinda, I'd had the opportunity to travel to the United States. I lived in upstate New York in the water shed (catchment) of New York City, and saw firsthand how important it is to conserve water. That's where some of my ideas for incorporating integrated water cycle management into our landscapes started to form.

When I got back to Australia I spent some time in the Dandenongs, and it reminded me how much I love this mountain, so close to Melbourne. There's also a wonderful community here. At the time I bought the property, I was a frustrated designer. I was finding it hard to communicate my vision of what *could* be done. I realised people needed to see examples so they could understand what I was talking about.

My selection criteria for buying a property were pretty specific: I wanted to have the best possible soil, a high rainfall, a bush block, views and, if possible, creek frontage. I managed to find all these things at Olinda. The soil is a red volcanic or mountain soil, and it's regarded as some of the best soil in Australia. It's unbelievably fertile.

When people see a backyard like mine they automatically perceive it as being something they can't have. One of the most important things I try to communicate as a designer is that we *can* translate and build these ecosystems in urban environments. People are yearning for this connection back to nature, and you really can build it anywhere.

On a waterfall tour of the United States I'd seen Frank Lloyd Wright's Fallingwater, the house he built over a waterfall in Pennsylvania. Can you believe he actually built a house on the edge of a waterway? He designed that residence to connect beautifully with nature. It inspired me to try to build my own waterfalls next to my house. And I've been able to achieve this without impacting on a waterway system; this project has shown you can utilise the run-off from the driveway to create a spectacular waterfall.

The team and I built the landscape in two stages: the lower billabong and the upper billabong. This was a very challenging site to work on. It's an extremely steep location and it was an ambitious build. We brought in truckloads of locally sourced material—rock, soil, fill, mulch—delivered by reversing down a steep driveway and passing underneath the house. What I learnt here helped

— — — —

'I wanted to have the best possible soil, a high rainfall, a bush block, views and, if possible, creek frontage. I managed to find all these things at Olinda.'

— — — —

———

Previous pages
Our signature curved boardwalk slicing through the natural pool. The house is surrounded by a natural amphitheatre of *Eucalyptus regnans* (giant mountain ash). *Dicksonia antarctica* (tree fern) is actually growing within the beached shallow areas of the natural pool. The ladder leaning against the boardwalk allows for easy access.

Opposite
Early morning reflections on the still water of the lower billabong. The only disturbance comes from ripples created by the native silver perch. This is the perfect growing climate for tree ferns. In the distance there are also understorey plantings of *Acacia melanoxylon* (Australian blackwood).

us enormously when we were at the Chelsea Flower Show in 2013. Chelsea was three times more complicated than what we built here, but Olinda is where it all started.

There's a 22 metre level change from the top of my studio to the base of the landscape, so we had gravity on our side. This allowed us to move and channel water beautifully throughout the landscape as the level changed. These multiple waterfalls create a curtain of water even when it rains, instead of going through a pipe and disappearing—you don't even need to turn a pump on! At Olinda, I worked with the contours of the land, looking for where the water came in and then identifying the best place to position the billabong.

The team and I worked with gravity to pipe the waterfalls—in fact, we try to work with gravity in all our projects. We tell our clients not to turn their waterfalls on all day, as there's simply no need. We still install pumps so they can be turned on when it's not raining; then, when it rains, nature fills up the billabong and the waterfall starts working.

In the same way I used to explore waterways when I was a kid, my children are drawn to the water flowing through the property, and the way it moves. They love to play among the rocks and streams.

I've designed Olinda so it draws you down into it. I learnt so much just by *doing*: how to place rocks, understanding logistics, working with highly trained excavator operators, the skills of project management and how you can execute a build on an extremely steep site, where safety is paramount.

Every single piece of stone at Olinda has been craned strategically into location. I'm really particular about stone placement. Each individual rock has been hand selected, and I've made sure it's the right piece of rock to use in the right location to create the right effect, whether that's for a waterfall, stepping stones, stones for sitting, keystones, diving boards or retaining rocks. For this landscape to be functional it needed significant rock retaining. There are descending stone staircases that connect the different spaces together.

I also wanted to show a range of different rocks. And I wanted to utilise local rock that was sourced less than 20 kilometres from home. At the lower section of the landscape we have a hornfels rock, which is quite angular. I wanted the angular shape because every single rock had to be strung up by a crane and moved to that location. We had rock barriers set up to avoid rocks rolling, but there was still the potential for danger—and if you sling up a round rock, it's more prone to slipping. So that's why we chose these angular rocks. At the top of our garden we've used bronze granite. Some people say you shouldn't mix types of stone, but ironically these rocks come from the same quarry—this is what can occur in nature.

It might sound strange, but when you work so much with rock you can read the rock, you can feel the rock, you develop an understanding with the rock. I really feel that the rock will tell you how it wants to be placed, how it wants to be connected with the earth. I would even say that it will place itself. So you need to study it and observe the way the rock wants to be positioned. And once again Mother Nature is the best reference. You need to do it thoughtfully. Look around you: next time you go to a natural environment where there's rock, look

at it. See how the plants grow around it, and how much of the rock is buried. Nature is amazing. We work so hard to create an artificial environment that looks like it's naturally been here forever!

At Olinda we don't have mains water. Moving here forced me to put in rainwater tanks and water-efficient appliances. I also installed first-flush rain diverters: when it rains, water hits the roof and goes into the gutter; if it hasn't rained in a while, there might be sediment in the gutters, so the first 100 litres are flushed into the garden, or a dry creekbed, before the fresh water enters the tank.

We built the infrastructure to collect water not only off the roof but also from the driveway. When we constructed the house we had to put two significant cuts into the landscape, and that altered the contours and the flow of water on the property. As soon as you put in a driveway you alter the flow of water off the landscape, even on flat sites. So I then had to manage a massive stormwater run-off issue. Up here in the Dandenong Ranges, since we're on such a steep site, stormwater run-off can build up momentum and become a significant problem. All the stormwater run-off is captured in the two billabongs—if it wasn't, it would go to one spot and saturate the soil profile, putting its structural integrity at risk. That could cause possible landslip issues or allow for those big mountain ashes to uproot. I was also blown away by the amount of water I could capture—we have between 900 and 1200 millimetres of rainfall a year.

After we won Best in Show at Chelsea in 2013, my wife saw what we had created and wondered if we could do that at Olinda. So in the months after Chelsea I embarked on converting our billabong into a natural pool. We're forever evolving our techniques, and here at home is where I practise—so I jumped at the opportunity. It would have been easier to put in an industry-standard chlorinated pool, but that's not true to my environmental philosophy.

As soon as I started using a billabong as a swimming pool, I had to rethink everything. I had to fence it to meet council regulations and make sure the water was being cleaned. We're now able to incorporate filtration systems that use microfibre technology, where good bacteria grow and assist in cleaning and purifying the water. My ideal scenario is to have a natural pool that fluctuates seasonally, but in such a manner that the whole system can still function and the water is cleaned in a biological way. We're getting there.

I had to install underwater filtration zones, which consisted of layers of different sizes of aggregate in addition to the microfibre technology. The body of water supports thousands of tadpoles and a whole range of aquatic life. By creating an ecosystem in these billabongs, it means there's no stagnant water—it's not a breeding ground for mosquitoes.

We developed ease-of-access points and shelves; for example, 50 centimetres below water level there are multiple stone slabs that make it easier to get in and out, and where you can sit. I also installed a small ladder similar to the one we used in the Chelsea garden. However, what my eldest son loves most of all is playing in the shallow beachy area.

You can jump off a 2.5 metre waterfall ledge into the pool—and it just brings back that sense of being a child. Even my father, on his seventieth birthday, has jumped off it! But what I really love is swimming up to the base of the waterfalls

The clarity of the natural pools is remarkable—you can easily see the river pebbles. It looks like a natural mountain stream. The ripples and movement on the water and the bubbles on the surface create a lovely visual effect.

Opposite
I swim up to the base of the waterfall and allow the water to spill over me. As we were building this, we designed secure planting pockets to enable tree ferns to grow through the nooks and crannies.

and letting the water cascade over my body. It's one of the most cleansing and energising experiences. I also built a small pebble path, which is really quite sensual when you walk over it in bare feet. It provides you with a reflexology experience prior to entering the body of water.

A beautifully constructed curved boardwalk separates the shallow beach area for children's play from the deep waterhole section. It's an interesting architectural form that slices through the natural pool. The timber ladder leans up against the boardwalk to allow ease of access. It was built by my old schoolteacher Brendan Stemp, who also made the ladder for Chelsea.

I've also built a spa, my Australian version of a hot spring, inspired by the Japanese *onsen*. I've designed little ledges for beer or wine glasses. You can see the beautiful craftsmanship of the stonework around the edges.

I live in a cool-temperate wet-sclerophyll rainforest. The upper storey is *Eucalyptus regnans* and the understorey is *Dicksonia antarctica* and *Cyathea australis*—soft and rough tree ferns. Ferns are a huge part of my life. My parents had ferneries, my grandparents had ferneries. They're such prehistoric, spectacular plants.

I'm quite amazed by how tree ferns have a dormant mechanism to deal with extreme situations such as fire and heat; they're even able to grow semi-submerged in water. Over the last few years, I've noticed how many tree ferns around our property have not been coping with the extreme heat we've been experiencing. I can't do much about this. Sometimes we get temperatures of up to 45°C here. But the ferns do come back to life.

A few of our neighbours talk about how beautiful the mountain is during the full moon, because when it's the full moon out here, the ferns just glow! My favourite things to artificially light within my landscape are the tree ferns. I like to illuminate the tree fern adjacent to our bedroom by shooting the light from the base up through the fronds. The silhouette creates the most stunning pattern on the ceiling of our bedroom.

I planted many tree ferns at Olinda, but I also worked around a lot of existing ones as part of the build process. I've got ferns that are over 200 hundred years old on our property. And I've really enjoyed watching how they naturally propagate themselves if you have the right damp environment.

Our stone steps are a great feature. I can see how they will look in the future. When you walk up them in fifty or 100 years' time, the numerous snow gums (*Eucalyptus pauciflora*) will have created a natural canopy above—a twisted, gnarled, sculptural canopy. Over time I've been weighing down some of the branches to assist in distorting the form of the tree. This practice is against all my arboricultural training principles, but what I've come to observe on my property is that everything wants to grow 70–90 metres tall! The snow gums are growing to reach the sunlight. So I have had to distort the elongation that would naturally occur. I've tried to stunt the trees to prevent them from growing straight up, and that creates more of an interesting habit and trunk formation.

When you live in an extremely fire-prone area such as the Dandenong Ranges you cannot ever be blasé. It's not a matter of if one will come, it's when.

— — — —

'I also built a small pebble path, which is really quite sensual when you walk over it in bare feet. It provides a reflexology experience prior to entering the body of water.'

— — — —

Opposite
Imagine jumping from the top of the waterfall into the pool! The hot spring has been placed next to the natural pool. Behind it is the solar panel, located in the best position to maximise the sun throughout the day. Young *Cyathea* are growing through the rocky alcoves. We have created the perfect microclimate for fern spores to germinate.

If you're living in a bush environment you must be prepared. It is crucial to have more water available in case of fire. I learnt early on that the most important part of your fire-prevention plan is to protect your fire pump, because that pump is like your heart. It must be protected from heat and flame.

We have fire sprinklers all over the roof of the house, which in the event of a fire will create a curtain of water. And I have to stress this has not been tested in a fire storm yet. The sprinklers are wetting an inner ring and an outer ring, not just the house, creating a damp circle around the property. And the great thing is the water then drains back into our billabongs, which will assist in prolonging our available water supply.

Olinda is the most complicated and challenging design I've ever done. I found coming up with the right one for this property to be an extremely complicated process. The first concept I developed was on a piece of scrap paper, and it evolved from there. You might develop a solid concept but, really, the design evolves when you're sculpting the landscape. In addition to the steep site conditions, the need to maximise sunlight was the main concern. We wanted to build terraces that optimise the available sunlight at certain times of the year.

We've integrated the solar panels at the most appropriate locations for capturing the sun, and ironically these are positioned within the landscape, rather than on the roof as they usually would be. Recent research has shown that surrounding the underside of solar power panels with plants increases the efficiency of the cell. I also find the placement of the solar panels makes it easier to clean them, rather than having to climb onto your roof to get to them.

As you come down through the spiral staircase that is surrounded by large tree ferns, you reach the outdoor hot shower. This has been handcrafted from an *Acacia dealbata* (silver wattle) off the property, and the handle has been creatively sculpted from a piece of mistletoe.

We also have a terraced vegetable patch where we grow a range of herbs throughout the year as well as kale, rocket, tomatoes, rhubarb and silverbeet. Here on Olinda the amount of good available sunlight necessary for growing vegetables is very limited. My dream would be to incorporate a rooftop vegetable garden, because the roof always has the best sunlight on a property.

When I first built this landscape I was going through a difficult phase in my life, and building it and putting my energy into something creative helped me through that phase. I call the lower billabong the healing pond. Putting your energy into creating something beautiful can help you get through grief. I am under a lot of pressure at times, and I live a pretty intense life. The garden really gives me a sense of balance.

Olinda was the inspiration for our Best in Show-winning garden at the Chelsea Flower Show in 2013 and I hope that in some way it helped change the way people view Australian native gardens.

What really motivated me to build this garden was wanting to create a beautiful environment in which to bring up a family. I was brought up to love being in the garden. Now watching my sons, William and Angus, they're learning the same thing. I can see how much they love it and that's what creating these landscapes is all about.

Opposite
Clockwise from top left: *Cyathea australis*; Detail of the unfurling new growth of a leaf frond; This garden is magical to walk through in the mornings, when light plays through the patterns of fern fronds; Detail of the tips of fronds of *Dicksonia antarctica*.

The outdoor hot shower. The pipeworks are concealed within the sculpted *Acacia dealbata* shower post. The flick mixer has been sculpted from mistletoe.

Opposite
Top: The majority of the *Cyathea australis* grows in the waterfall.

Bottom: A private sitting area with a firepit. From a design viewpoint, it is important to have sitting areas in the garden other than the patio. This is one of my favourite views of my garden.

A great example of phototropism: this *Dicksonia antarctica* has developed a strong bend in its trunk, searching for sunlight. Who needs colour in a garden like this? The green is intense, and there are many varying shades, depending on the light. The tree fern fronds have evolved so that when a large branch falls from above, they easily break away to deflect damage away from the crown.

The following labels appear on the watercolour plan:

PUMP HOUSE 2

CINEMA SCREEN

STEPPING STONES

STEPPING STONES & SHOWER

SUN HAMMOCK

FIRE PUMP STATION & WATER TREATMENT PLANT

BILLABONG

OVER FLOW

ENTERTAINING & SEATING AREA FOR OUT DOOR CINEMA

WATER TANKS

CREEK

CREEK

OUT DOOR HEATED SHOWER

UPPER LEVEL DECKS

STEPPING STONES OVER CREEK

FIRE HOSE 1

RESIDENCE

FENCE

RETAINING WALL

RAMP

LOWER DRIVE SLIT PIT, DIRECTING STORM WATER TO BILLABONG

OUT DOOR FIRE

OVERFLOW TO LOWER BILLABONG

BILLABONG

DIVING ROCK

DECKING OVER PUMP HOUSE 1

DRAIN

OFFICE / WORK SHED

WATER TANK

Clockwise from above: Watercolour plan of the landscape design; The lower billabong, where every rock has been hand selected and carefully placed; A mixed planting of *Dichondra repens* and *Viola hederacea* creeps around the rock steps and creates a softening effect; A large rock has been positioned just behind the waterfall so you can sit and enjoy the surrounds; Young, recently germinated *Persicaria decipiens*—the root hairs assist in removing the nutrients from the natural pool.

'A beautifully constructed curved boardwalk separates the shallow beach area for children's play from the deep waterhole section. It's an interesting architectural form that slices through the natural pool. The timber ladder leans up against the boardwalk to allow ease of access.'

— — — — —

Left: The upper margin of the pool has a number of aquatic species growing, including a combination of *Juncus australis* and *Juncus gregiflorus*, *Triglochin striatum*, *Eleocharis sphacelata* and *Ranunculus glabrifolius*.

Below: This waterfall is able to create a curtain of water even when it rains. We work with gravity to pipe the waterfalls, so that when it rains, nature fills up the billabong and the waterfall starts flowing.

Bottom: *Persicaria decipiens* has been grown at the water's edge, softening the rocks of the billabong.

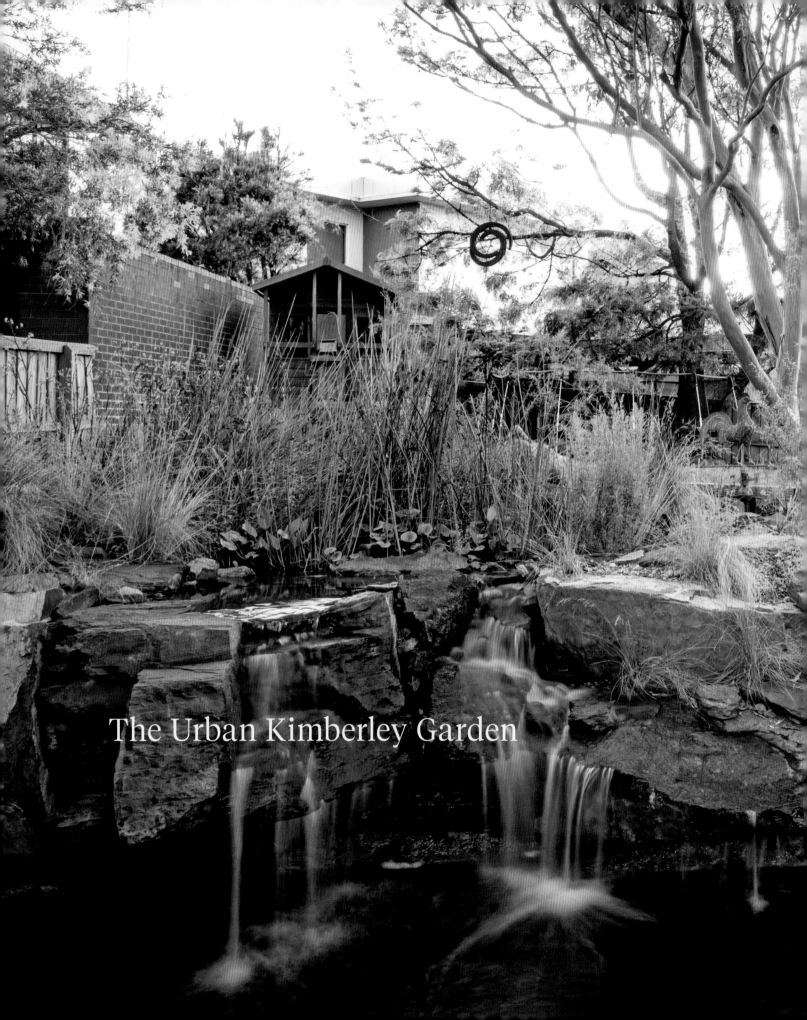

The Urban Kimberley Garden

The Urban Kimberley Garden

The owners of this property, Silke and Jeremy, loved the Kimberley region in Western Australia. They'd fallen in love with the area on a family holiday, and they wanted to bring the magic and meaningfulness of that landscape—especially the interaction of rocks and water—to their own garden in their bayside suburb of Victoria.

One of my aims is to bring beauty back to our urban environments. Everyone is familiar with the notion of going out into nature to revive and re-energise: we all go to national parks and visit breathtaking landscapes on our holidays, but then we come back to our cities. Why not create those beautiful environments at home?

Before this garden was built, there were a couple of established trees on the property, which we've retained, but other than that there was nothing out here except for weeds. One of the great things about this project was that the team and I were able to create the garden at the same time as the house was being built, so we could look at the designs of both and how they interrelated. The build took about two months, and we worked in stages.

The new residence has a smaller footprint than the one that used to be here, to maximise space and encourage more landscape and garden. Adding more space allows more permeability and also more green in an urban environment. What's happening in our cities is more subdivision and more hard non-permeable surfaces, so whenever we can increase the green space it's helping to improve the big picture.

This garden allowed us as designers to create lots of different spaces or 'rooms', and there are various spots throughout the garden where you can stop and sit and enjoy the beauty.

As you enter the property, you immediately engage with nature; the path takes you around large slabs of mudstone, slowing you down after your hard day and allowing you to engage with the landscape. So it's not just a straight path, it's an experience. You step over plantings of herbs and the aroma stimulates your senses. We've planted some rosemary and thyme by the door, so as you walk in you can break off a bunch for your evening roast. That creates a really sensual experience from the outset. You then go up a little mound and through an orchard where we've planted the fruit trees in a random arrangement.

When we design a space we look at available light and water: where is the best source of light to grow things? For example, before the construction of the new house, there was a driveway where the orchard now grows. You should zone your planting according to the plants' light requirements in order to maximise photosynthesis. This design thinking also applies to irrigation requirements and, again, we zone planting accordingly. What this means is: don't plant plants that require a lot of water next to plants that need little water. All plants that require the same amount of water are grouped together.

We wanted produce to be a prominent part of this garden. I believe every garden should incorporate some element of growing its own fruit and

Previous pages
An adventure playground set in a natural Australian urban backyard, encompassing a billabong complete with rocky gorge.

Opposite
The front garden features plants such as *Myoporum parvifolium*, *Poa labillardieri*, *Correa alba*, *Xanthorrhoea johnsonii* and *X. minor*, and *Corymbia ficifolia* 'Baby Scarlet'.

vegetables. This family harvest their own stone fruit, apples and citrus. The orchard also serves to link the front and rear garden areas, and screens the property from the neighbours. The trees aren't planted in an avenue or against the fence line; the plants dictate their own meandering pathway. This type of planting slows you down as you come through the garden, encouraging you to move in and among the plants, to engage with the landscape as you enter the space. You can even grab a piece of fruit to eat on the way.

Silke and Jeremy were clear about their vision, both for right now and as their children grow. An important aspect was encouraging the kids to get out into the garden, and to draw them into the landscape. Silke gave me some good ideas on designing gardens for children. She taught me how important the children's experience of the flow of play throughout the landscape is. As you walk through the garden you're going on a journey. Through our design we've got the children playing, sitting on rocks, helping to harvest vegetables and exploring.

There was an old tree out the front that the owners wanted to retain, but sadly it died during the build of the house. So we suggested: why not just take it into the backyard? The owners loved the idea because it's such a natural way to have kids' climbing equipment without having climbing equipment! We simply dragged it into the backyard, and it works well. The lawn area is also a great spot for children to play in. We created it so that it features a bit of 'movement'—it's not just a flat plane.

You can see that it's a children's garden, an interactive garden and a habitat, with a tapestry of textures and interest to keep young people of all ages engaged. Playing with imagination was really important, incorporating a sense of adventure that allows the children to explore, to have life experiences in the garden, and to connect to the beauty of nature. As you can see, there are tracks that meander and rocky little ledges to sit on. The owners' children spend hours in it every day.

We've used the indigenous flora of this bayside region throughout the suburban property to create a sustainable landscape with visual interest. We've planted coastal grasses and pig face (*Carpobrotus glaucescens*). What we're trying to do is mimic Mother Nature as much as possible.

Silke had grown up with a pond in her backyard in Germany, and in our early discussions she described to me how as a young girl she loved watching the ducks fly in, having birds flock to the garden to drink all year round, and looking for tadpoles. Similarly, a billabong is so much the soul of a landscape, it's the centre of everything, and Silke and her family wanted one because it would draw more fauna to the garden. The billabong is a gathering spot for the whole family in the afternoons. It's also a haven for birds and dragonflies. There's nothing better than sitting in a garden and watching the habitat come alive.

One of the interesting features of this garden is the curved entertainment deck. It's made out of radial sawn timber. I love working with curves; I like the transition from the angular achitecture to the organic and freeflowing landscape. The inspiration for the curved deck was our Melbourne International Flower and Garden Show 2009 sunset platform design. Silke saw

— — — —

'We've used the indigenous flora of this bayside region throughout the suburban property to create a sustainable landscape with visual interest.'

— — — —

Opposite
Top: The backyard, featuring the *Eucalyptus pauciflora*—with its sculptural trunk.

Bottom: The deck opens out onto the billabong and creates a beautiful transition from the formal, modern architecture to the natural, informal garden. It connects the house and garden in a really fluid way.

it and loved the feel of it and wanted us to do the same thing here. The deck opens out onto the billabong and creates a really beautiful transition from the formal, contemporary architecture to the natural, informal, organic garden. It connects the house and garden in a really fluid way.

The integrated water management system here is impressive. The only tap that is connected to the mains water system is the one at the kitchen sink, which they use for drinking—the rest of the house runs on rainwater. And that's what I try to encourage people to do. I believe we should only be using mains water for drinking. Not for flushing toilets or for irrigation. Silke and Jeremy's property is a testament to how this works, for a family of five, in a suburban, bayside home. This system is applicable to new builds and to existing homes, and it could be the future of every suburban household in the world. It's all about devising a solution for each property. Certainly it's an additional expense, but you will save money in the long run, and help the environment.

Underneath the lawn is a big water tank that holds 23,000 litres and provides almost all the water required for the house. This tank collects all the roof water, which then overflows into the billabong. The owners haven't watered the garden, apart from the veggie patch, for the last four years.

The garden is such a fun, energising space. We've made a chicken area at the back and the owners have installed a flying fox from their rooftop. As with all my landscapes, I wanted to use materials from the site where possible. Being involved in the early planning of the property meant we were able to reuse the existing topsoil from the site as well as other excavated material. We then sculpted it to create interesting contours and forms within the landscape.

Often I come to a property and find that it's been completely flattened: there's no shape or definition, no form or movement or beauty within the landscape. And that's what the team and I aim to bring back. It annoys me when the topsoil is taken away while a house is being built—when it comes time to landscape, you have to buy your soil back from the garden suppliers. This is ludicrous! Just remember, the soil on your property should be treated like gold, because often you can't buy back soil anywhere near as good.

The mounds in the garden direct water to certain points, by moving the water through the contours of the landscape. For example, on the top of a mound you can plant really drought-resistant plants, and where that mound might meet a swale you can grow more water-tolerant plants.

We used granitic sand paths to provide access through the garden. This topping creates a comfortable walkway for barefoot children. We've varied the widths of the paths to create a depth of space, and plants are strategically placed throughout the gravel, so that now we're getting self-seeded new plants growing up out of it.

Silke and Jeremy built their own veggie garden from reclaimed bricks from the property. It's raised up, but instead of having neat little beds, the design is twisted. It also creatively incorporates reclaimed cages from the old Leggo's pasta sauce factory; they're the cages they used to transport the cans in. This provides a structure to grow certain climbers on.

Opposite
Clockwise from top left: The curved deck provides the perfect place to sit, relax and observe the garden; An old tree trunk was reused as a seat or balancing log for the kids, and granitic sand was used for a permeable surface; The veggie patch was built using bricks recycled from the old driveway—flowing curves maximise the space; *Poa poiformis* merging through the vertical fence built from recycled railway sleepers.

Clockwise from above: Upper billabong planted with a mix of indigenous aquatics such as *Lythrum salicaria*, *Alisma plantago-aquatica*, *Nymphoides* sp., *Myriophyllum crispatum* and *Mentha australis*. Mudstone rocks were craned in and made into this waterfall, which looks like it has been there forever. *Eleocharis sphacelata* in foreground; The mudstone rocks hold pools of water that the children like to touch, play and connect with; Simple plantings of *Dichondra repens* and *Poa poiformis* throughout the steps create a very tactile experience when walking through the pathways.

The family love rocks, and we've designed the garden so that the rock flows through the property in a north-easterly direction, like faultlines of stone, bringing back memories of those trips to the Kimberley region. The faultline runs in a very natural and organic way and creates smaller, distinct areas. The stones emerge out of the soil mounds on gentle angles and contribute a very sculptural feeling to the space, and they allow for beautiful planting pockets throughout.

You can see how leaves are falling from the trees and natural recycling is occurring, and that's important in an urban environment. The last thing you want to do is take your leaf matter away, when this can actually replenish your soils with nutrients and also assist in retaining soil moisture. I remember my grandparents being adamant about clearing leaves from their garden as soon as they fell, but now we understand the importance of recycling nutrients, even if those leaves are collected and composted so that the fallen leaves go back into the garden.

I think it's this type of garden that should be the norm for the Australian backyard. It has produce, play areas, a billabong, and a whole integrated water cycle management system underlying it. I hope it inspires people to think carefully about their own backyards and how they can make them both practical and a source of enjoyment, while at the same time ensuring they are environmentally responsible.

'I think it's this type of garden that should be the norm for the Australian backyard. It has produce, play areas, a billabong, and a whole integrated water cycle management system ...'

The beauty in the placement of the rocks directs the flow of the water, creating wonderful effects.

Opposite
Clockwise from top left:
Anigozanthos flavidus 'Bush Gold'; *Ficinia nodosa*; *Acacia glaucoptera*; *Rosmarinus officinalis*.

An Indigenous Garden

An Indigenous Garden

This property, once a 1920s sewage pumping station, is on a parcel of land that was subdivided in the early 2000s. It's located about 5 kilometres from the centre of the Melbourne CBD, on the banks of the Yarra River.

The owners wanted a low-maintenance garden that would be self-sustaining and require minimal irrigation. Their vision for what could be accomplished had to abide by council requirements. To help preserve biodiversity in the area, one of the local Boroondara Council restrictions was that the garden had to be strictly indigenous. There were planting requirements and a list that needed to be adhered to. It also had to have minimal hard surfacing and a stormwater management system.

There's a difference between the definitions of native plants and indigenous plants. Indigenous species are defined as plants that are specifically adapted to a local area: to the rainfall, the soil conditions and the extremities of that environment. Whereas native plants exist throughout the whole country. For example, a particular eucalypt might grow here, but it won't actually exist a kilometre around the bend—it is located only on this little parcel of land. And that's what made this project so fascinating.

The land slopes steeply and dramatically down to the Yarra River—the property at road level is 29 metres above sea level, and then it drops to 17 metres. The river was an incredible backdrop to work with and attach our design to. We wanted to create a wildlife corridor that went all the way down to the river and connected with the existing landscape. There were remnant river red gums (*Eucalyptus camaldulensis*) surrounding the property, so it was also important to work with the existing vegetation.

This is one of the most complicated builds the team and I have done, just because of the logistics of trying to work in such a confined, steep and suburban location. The slope of the land was a great challenge. We had to work with it, rather than fight it. The natural topography of the land here inspired a series of waterfalls and billabongs.

There are two billabongs, an upper and a lower. We created the two billabongs in order that the water could be pumped around and create an impressive waterfall. We wanted to get the water level of the upper billabong as high as possible, to floor level, so it could be viewed from the living space and, like the Yarra River, was right at the back door. The lower billabong has been set to the highest flood-level marker. The construction took three months to complete, and an extraordinary amount of retaining was required.

Getting the rocks in without damaging them was difficult. You have to be extremely cautious, because you want them to remain as natural and undamaged as possible. And because they're going to be situated within the landscape for a long time, you have to place them with care.

These types of gardens probably best suit the low-maintenance approach. If you create the right environment, the plants within it will self-seed and assist in recruiting and regenerating new plants. You don't need to water. This garden

— — — —

'We wanted to create a wildlife corridor that went all the way down to the river and connected with the existing landscape.'

— — — —

Previous pages
Eucalyptus camaldulensis behind the upper billabong. An extensive mixture of indigenous plants were used around this billabong.

Opposite
A play of reflections helps connect the landscape to the building. The internal cavity of the stone wall pipes the stormwater from the roof to the billabong. This assists in sustaining the garden.

has a habitat corridor leading down to the Yarra, and it brings in the local fauna. The billabong links the water of the Yarra right up to the house. It's not about treating the garden as a separate entity, it's about being considerate to the surrounding landscape and becoming a part of it.

We were able to channel the water with the use of gravity down through the landscape. Just as they do at Olinda, the waterfalls will also come alive when it rains, without the need of a pump.

All the rainwater is directed to the rainwater tank and is then redirected into the billabongs. In peak flow, after everything is replenished, it will overflow to the Yarra River. The water bill for this property has remained under the minimum for two people since the installation of the rainwater tank. Even during the drought, the owners never watered the garden.

The steps, which are made of sedimentary stone, invite you to explore the garden. Halfway up there's a little sitting rock that allows you to settle on the edge of the waterfall to look down over the river. We also wanted to create an experience with the steps, and we did this by changing the angles so that as you travel up and down you're moving through the landscape.

We've created lots of little perching points for birds and frogs and lizards. I positioned a sculptural piece of log adjacent to the billabong and it's become a favourite landing spot for kookaburras and other kingfishers. The birds love it. The property also attracts rosellas, lorikeets, yellow-tailed black cockatoos, honeyeaters, finches, wagtails and wrens. Not to mention butterflies, frogs and water dragons! The owners have even had a young wallaby come up to the back door.

People often ask me how the frogs know to appear once we've built a billabong. They notice that one day they have water in the billabong and the next day they have frogs. I describe it as kind of like this: imagine your house is the only house in the world. It would be easy for other people to find. We'd be drawn to the comfortable living room, the sustaining food and produce in the kitchen, the electricity and warmth and shelter the house offers. And that's what the billabong is like. It's got protection—nooks and crannies where the frogs can hide; and it's got *Triglochin*, a water ribbon that is the perfect frog habitat, a plant in which they lay their eggs. The billabong provides a healthy ecosystem, and we've mimicked their perfect habitat, so of course they will come! Just have patience. I love when I get a phone call from an owner saying the first frogs have arrived.

The owners of this indigenous garden enjoy sitting on their deck and watching the cycle of the day. They've noticed how the birds behave according to a timetable. In the early morning the finches come for a bath, then it's the rosellas for a quick feed and a swim before disappearing. In the afternoon the kookaburras come in for a quick hello and a dip in the billabong. And then the frogs start.

The owners find they're spending more time in their garden now, and that's exactly what we set out to achieve.

Opposite
Clockwise from top left: Upper waterfall; *Wahlenbergia stricta*, *Chrysocephalum semipapposum*, a mixture of *Poa* species and *Austrostipa scabra* subsp. *falcata*; *Triglochin procerum*—my favourite water plant; Lorikeets visit the garden daily.

Top: *Pycnosorus globosus*, also known as Billy buttons. This was the first flower I gave my wife.

Bottom: The late afternoon sun creates a lovely light filtering through the indigenous grasses and reflecting on the rocks and water.

Opposite
Boulders were placed throughout to create different forms and depths—great for rock hopping! Logs were positioned to help create a habitat.

'The steps, which are made of sedimentary stone, invite you to explore the garden. Halfway up there's a little sitting rock that allows you to settle on the edge of the waterfall to look down over the Yarra River.'

Big retaining rocks were used. This granite is surrounded by plants, with *Lythrum salicaria* in bud.

Opposite:
The stepping stones make you want to explore and see what is beyond, bringing out the adventurer in us all. A mix of indigenous aquatics has been planted here.

Following pages
Poa labillardieri with rocks in the background.

The Rock Garden

The Rock Garden

Set amid the stunning Strathbogies in country Victoria, this property occupies 400 acres (162 hectares). The surrounding landscape is rocks, rocks and more rocks! But at some time in the past, an area of the property had been stripped of all its rocks. They had been pushed to the side to make way for sheep grazing or for a lawn, and out of all the original stone just one enormous 150 tonne piece of granite remained on the site—which we kept as part of the new garden.

When the current owners arrived, the area was an extremely tired, worked landscape. All that remained were some weeds, so our aim was to bring it all back and revive this landscape. We really wanted to try to replicate the natural environment.

We relocated for the build and brought in a team of construction people and a horticulturalist to focus solely on this project, which took three months of very hard work. It is one of the bigger projects we've been involved in.

This is such an extreme environment. There's significant level change on the land, around 8 metres. The geography of the land means that the property sits in a rain shadow, so any rain that does fall nearby misses the property anyway. The average rainfall around here is about 600 millimetres for the whole year, but when we started building this garden in the heart of the drought in 2008 they were getting much less than that—under 300 millimetres for the whole year. A critical element of our design brief was to create a landscape that would survive in these severe conditions.

The owners' livelihood revolves around their organic olive grove, so the landscape we've designed is secondary to that—any available water must be used for irrigating the olives and other produce. The landscape has to survive on its own without any irrigation. It also has to be extremely low maintenance, so we selected a lot of indigenous plants that are used to the tough conditions. I proposed mimicking the rock placement that already existed elsewhere near the property, and which had possibly originally been a feature of this site.

We created a billabong that decentralises all the water that comes off the driveway, so that it can be used for irrigation. When the billabong overflows, the water is piped to the dam, and then the dam water is used to irrigate the olives. Not a drop is wasted.

We wanted to store as much water as possible, so it was critical to make the billabong a good depth. As we dug we kept hitting massive boulders, some the size of a 4WD, and there was no way we were going to move them! And so the shape of the billabong was created out of the conditions, out of working around existing rock formations, and we made that a feature, adapting the design as we went.

The billabong also, importantly, assists in providing fire protection. Having a large surface area of water on the northern side of the property—the direction a fire would probably come from—creates a non-combustible no-flame zone. But it's important to be aware that extreme weather and fire events can alter the direction of the flame, meaning the danger could actually come from

Previous pages
A lichen-covered boulder weighing over 150 tonnes is the entry point to the Rock Garden.

Opposite
A view of the billabong. Plant species include *Eleocharis sphacelata, Lythrum salicaria* and *Melaleuca armillaris*. In the billabong we've planted *Nymphoides* sp., an aquatic flowering plant.

We created different paths through the garden, allowing the owners to enjoy every aspect.

anywhere. The billabong is also fitted with local fire authority access points. The fire sprinklers can function without the use of a pump, just through the use of the head pressure in the water tank approximately 100 metres above the property.

We built this landscape during one of the driest years on record, and the billabong filled up that year with just the small amount of rain that fell. It shows you don't need a lot of water to maintain this sort of system.

We can apply these same principles to every urban environment. Conserving water shouldn't just be a rural principle. We have to think about both flood mitigation and conserving water. Flood mitigation means slowing down the stormwater surge and avoiding putting excess demands on our existing stormwater infrastructure. And surviving during drought is about holding and retaining that water, storing it to use it throughout the year when required.

This property has no mains power or mains water; everything is running off solar panels. So we wanted any pumps we used to be the most energy-efficient choices. The approach I try to encourage is not just to think about your garden when it comes to water and energy efficiency.

In our build we tried to use mostly local materials. The rock came from stockpiles off the property, the soil came from the site and the gravel came from just around the corner. The only thing we brought in was plumbing materials—a couple of pumps and waterproof membranes.

We've had to be strategic in the way we blended the property's exotic gardens with the indigenous. It's like a French provincial garden on the edge of the Strathbogies. It flows together seamlessly.

The property now looks like it's been there forever. And that should be the aim of a sustainable landscape: that it fits well within the local environment.

As you walk into the garden you pass some environmental weeds, the agapanthus, which the owner promises me she dead-heads every season to reduce the spread (they can be quite invasive). Then you transition into the more native and indigenous garden where we had to work around some established lemon-scented gums (*Corymbia citriodora*).

There are a lot of indigenous plants here, but some of them have struggled during the establishment phase, because of the extreme weather conditions. The owners only watered in the very beginning, by using a very elaborate irrigation method—a watering can dipped into the billabong! And if the plants didn't adapt, then they had no chance.

The owners' lifestyle revolves around sitting out next to the billabong. Breakfast and lunch are eaten outdoors every day. And the sunsets are spectacular— a wonderful pink glow in the landscape. The garden attracts lots of bird life: finches, wrens and honeyeaters. The owners watch them dive bomb into the billabong. They have about five species of frogs, too.

It's really important that you design a billabong in proportion to the space. We had this large blank canvas to work with, so, from a design perspective, we needed a large body of water. The size of the billabong is also determined by the

available water we can collect to fill and replenish. I am often asked by people how to fill these billabongs ... You wait for it to rain!

Creating a habitat within a billabong like this can actually be instant. Once it rains and the billabong fills, you'll find that frogs and tadpoles, and then birds, start visiting. We've planted indigenous aquatic plants to certain depth requirements to stop root growth and spread.

The length within the billabong enabled us to create lovely enclosed vistas. We always design a whole landscape so that you can experience it at different times of the day. Functionality is also very important, especially with properties of this size.

The principles we've used here can be applied to an urban environment, because we all need to conserve water no matter where we live. Even in the suburbs, we know the drought is going to come again because it's a cycle. And that's why I believe water conservation is crucial—because you are future-proofing your property in order to have available water in times of drought as well as flood. These systems are basically about designing landscapes that will be sustainable in Australian conditions.

Opposite
Top: The rock stockpile on the property, which we could use.

Bottom: The waterfall here works beautifully with the natural flow of the land.

The play of light and the reflections on the surface of the water in the billabong show how our gardens add so much dimension. The length of the billabong allowed us to create lovely enclosed vistas.

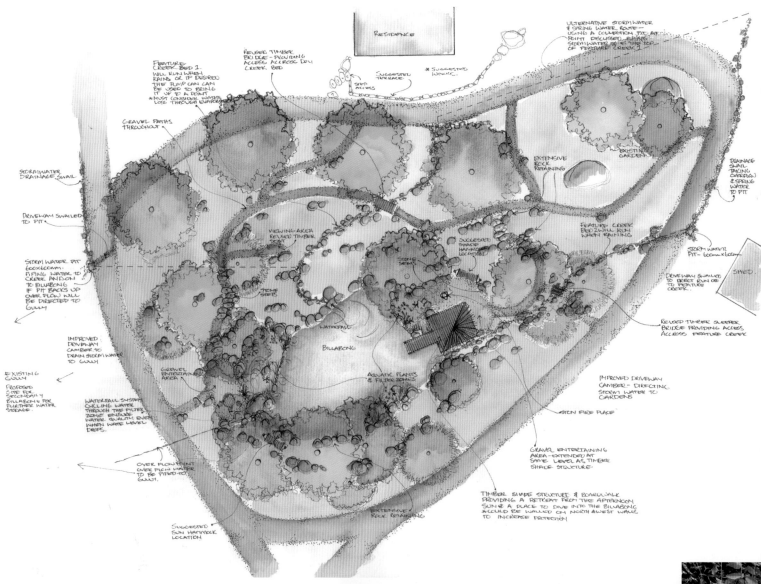

RESIDENCE

ALTERNATIVE STORMWATER & SPRING WATER ROUTE — USING A COLLECTION PIT AT POINT DISCUSSED. PIPING STORMWATER TO THE TOP OF FEATURE CREEK TO

FEATURE CREEK BED 1 WILL RUN WHEN IT RAINS OR IF DESIRED THE PUMP CAN CAN BE USED TO BRING IT UP TO A POINT * MUST CONSIDER WATER LOSS THROUGH EVAPORATION

REUSED TIMBER BRIDGE - PROVIDING ACCESS ACROSS DRY CREEK BED

SUGGESTED TERRACE

* SUGGESTED WALKS.

STEP ACCESS

GRAVEL PATHS THROUGHOUT

EXISTING GARDEN

EXTENSIVE ROCK RETAINING

STORMWATER DRAINAGE SWALE

DRIVEWAY SWAILED TO PIT.

VIEWING AREA REUSED TIMBER

DRAINAGE SWAIL TAKING OVERFLOW & SPRING WATER TO PIT

FEATURE CREEK BED 2 WILL RUN WHEN RAINING

SUGGESTED SHADE HAMMOCK LOCATION

STORM WATER PIT 600x600mm

STORM WATER PIT 600x600mm. PIPING WATER TO CREEK AND ON TO BILLABONG IF PIT BACKS UP OVER FLOW WILL BE DIRECTED TO GULLY

STONE SEATS

SHED

DRIVEWAY SWAILED TO DIRECT RUN OFF TO FEATURE CREEK

ZONE SEATS

WATERFALL

REUSED TIMBER SLEEPER BRIDGE PROVIDING ACCESS ACROSS FEATURE CREEK

IMPROVED DRIVEWAY CAMBER TO DRAIN STORM WATER TO GULLY

BILLABONG

AQUATIC PLANTS & FILTER ZONES

IMPROVED DRIVEWAY CAMBER - DIRECTING STORM WATER TO GARDENS

EXISTING GULLY

PROPOSED SITE FOR SECONDARY BILLABONG FOR FURTHER WATER STORAGE.

GRAVEL ENTERTAINING AREA

STONE FIRE PLACE

WATERFALL SYSTEM CIRCLING WATER THROUGH THE FILTER ZONE ENSURES WATER QUALITY EVEN WHEN WATER LEVEL DROPS.

GRAVEL ENTERTAINING AREA - EXTENDED AT SAME LEVEL AS TIMBER SHADE STRUCTURE.

OVER FLOW POINT OVER FLOW WATER TO BE PIPED TO GULLY.

TIMBER SHADE STRUCTURE & BOARDWALK PROVIDING A RETREAT FROM THE AFTERNOON SUN & A PLACE TO DIVE INTO THE BILLABONG & COULD BE WALLED ON NORTH & WEST WALLS TO INCREASE PROTECTION

SUGGESTED SUN HAMMOCK LOCATION

EXTENSIVE ROCK RETAINING

Clockwise from above: Watercolour plan of the Rock Garden. This shows the scale of the billabong compared to the house; This 150 tonne boulder provides great support for a rambling rose; A little creek where the rock placement creates a great environment for amphibians; Meandering curved stairs between strategically placed boulders; The waterfall here is really inconspicuous, mimicking what occurs within the surrounding natural environment. I wanted it to blend in with the landscape rather than be too overpowering. The waterfall is powered by solar panels installed on the property.

Clockwise from top left:
Eremophila decipiens; Acacia pycnantha; Corymbia citriodora; Rhagodia spinescens; Acacia pycnantha; Eremophila glabra; Rhagodia spinescens; Eremophila glabra grey leaf form. Centre: *Myoporum parvifolium.*

Opposite
Stunning play of reflections. Boulder poking its head through *Baloskion tetraphyllum.*

A Produce Garden

A Produce Garden

This suburban garden once consisted of lots of dead plants and a lawn that was also dying off. The owners, Rosemary and James, wanted to grow veggies in their backyard, but during the drought everything died. They were tired of looking out on their garden and seeing dead plants, so they decided they needed to develop something that was sustainable.

We had to work around three trees on the property that had been there for fifty-odd years: a manna gum (*Eucalyptus viminalis*) and two Sydney blue gums (*Eucalyptus saligna*). The owners felt like they were custodians of those trees. The trees are the assets of your property. Before we begin any project, we evaluate the trees. We look at the health, structure and form of each one, the location and suitability, and then we design around these things accordingly. Any trees on your property should be protected during a build. It's important to zone off the root system to avoid damage and compaction from digging with machinery during the construction phase. A particular issue on this property was that anything we planted under the three eucalypts would have to deal with the bushland confetti—leaves, twigs, bark, flowers, seed capsules—that fall from them constantly.

At the front of the house we built stepping stones to create a transition zone from the carport to the house. You can hear your shoes on the gravel as soon as you step out of the car, helping you feel instantly connected with the earth the minute you arrive home. Then you walk across a little boardwalk made of reclaimed timber and onto the irregular slate paving, which creates another transition and allows you to get the gravel off your feet before you go inside.

Along the side of the house, you wander down a meandering path of compacted granitic sand through to the back garden. Pretty much every surface here is permeable, allowing water to percolate back into the soil, providing soil moisture around the house for plants to access. It's really important to maintain some degree of soil moisture around the perimeter of a building, because it will prevent the soil and clay drying out too much. If clay is allowed to shrink and crack significantly it can cause structural damage to brick walls and foundations.

Four raised galvanised steel vegetable tanks are positioned along the western fence in order to capture maximum sun. I chose to use galvanised steel vegetable tanks because they are durable, easy to install, are a good height to work with and are really smart space-wise. The thin profile of the galvanised steel allows more space within the landscape. The owners grow tomatoes, kale and lettuce. Large reclaimed timber posts are placed adjacent to the tanks to support espaliered fruit trees. The brief was to grow as much produce as possible and to maximise the available growing space. The fruit trees also soften the otherwise plain timber paling fence. The owners grow apricots, plums, apples and nectarines, which they use to make jams and chutneys.

Around the house we've planted a herb garden featuring mint and rosemary. I like having herbs near the house so they're easy to access. Strawberry plants have been scattered throughout; they've self-propagated and now dot the

— — — —

'I encourage everyone in growing their own fruit and vegetables, because when you've participated in it and nurtured it, you know what's gone into the food you're eating.'

— — — —

Previous pages
The raised galvanised steel vegetable tanks are a feature of the garden.

Opposite
On either side of the waterfall there are dense plantings of *Baloskion tetraphyllum* and three *Eucalyptus pauciflora* subsp. *debeuzevillei* trees to add a multi-trunk effect.

pathways, meaning you can reach down and pick a strawberry as you move through the garden. I love incorporating that element of surprise into a landscape.

Produce is the key element in this garden. I encourage everyone to grow their own fruit and vegetables, because when you've participated in it and nurtured it, you know what's gone into the food you're eating. You've watched it evolve from a little seedling to what's on your plate, and you're connected to it. There's nothing better than eating a salad fresh from your garden.

Every component of this landscape works for the owners—it's not just a garden that's pretty to look at, it's a form of permaculture, a sustainable multi-use landscape. Behind the waterfall there's a firepit and a bench where the owners like to sit.

A curved deck of recycled timbers cantilevers over a small billabong. The beautiful waterfall is positioned so it can be viewed from within the house, and at night it's highlighted by soft lighting. A pump can be used to operate the waterfall, but it also runs naturally when it rains, using the overflow from the rainwater tanks. Next to no water exits the property—all of it is used on site.

When we create a waterfall, we design it in a way that makes it look like it's connected to the landscape. You don't want it to appear out of the blue. Getting the right effect does take some time. As an example, over the years I've recorded many man-made waterfalls around the world, and studied them to try to get the appropriate sound effect, something that's not displeasing to the ear. And here in this garden we've mounded up the earth so it actually flows into the height of the waterfall. In this way it's connecting with the landscape, and doesn't look like it's just been placed there artificially.

There's a lot of subdivision in this area of suburban Melbourne, where most of the rainwater is drained off each property. As a result, these suburbs have major issues with stormwater exiting people's land. However, when it rains in this garden, the water goes into the rainwater tanks first. The tanks are connected up to the house and the water is used within the home. The tanks overflow into the billabong and the billabong flows to the dry creekbed, and then eventually overflows to stormwater. A whole chain of events slows down the stormwater run-off.

It's just like the way a billabong works in nature: it's full of richness and diversity, so that when the rain arrives it fills up the billabong and all the seeds and good organisms float back downstream and help rejuvenate and heal different areas. By incorporating indigenous plants in the billabongs we create, we're reducing the spread of invasive aquatic weed into our waterways. These indigenous water plants also help reduce the amount of nutrient and nitrates that would normally go into the water supply. This helps to deliver healthy, higher-quality water back into our stormwater systems, because these plants assist in filtering it.

What's amazing about this property is that it doesn't rely on mains water. It has access to 'free' water. This is a way of future-proofing your property so that during periods of drought you have water available to irrigate your veggies. Our water is getting more expensive, but if you have a system like this, you can use

Clockwise from top left: *Acacia glaucoptera; Calothamnus quadrifidus* grey leaf form; Detail of *Calothamnus quadrifidus* grey leaf form; *Acacia cognata* 'Mini Cog'.

Opposite
Grevillea 'Bonfire'.

the saved rainwater to irrigate your garden and produce. And in times of flooding it slows the water down.

If you want to make a really simple start on incorporating water management systems such as this into your own backyard, the first thing to do is pay attention when it rains. When you get a serious downpour, observe what happens on your property. Grab an umbrella and watch where the stormwater goes. If you see it all go to a stormwater pipe—that's what we're trying to avoid. Start with installing a rainwater tank and connect one downpipe into it.

There's an extraordinary biodiversity in this backyard. There are around 120 different species of plants here. Wherever possible, I apply this philosophy of having as much diversity as we can in a landscape. One of my favourite eucalypts is the *Eucalyptus pauciflora* subsp. *debeuzevillei*, a type of snow gum, and we've planted three of them here, creating a multi-trunk effect. Its bark and trunk formation are extremely sculptural. We also wanted plants that attracted birds, butterflies and other insects, because they're important for pollination.

Another plant featured in this garden, *Lomandra patens*, has a wonderful structure and great architectural potential. It's butterfly-attracting and in the late evenings it also emits a subtle scent. There's lots of green, texture and foliage within this garden. You don't realise you're in suburbia.

Clockwise from above: The raised galvanised steel veggie tanks are a good height to work with and the thin profile of the steel allows more space within the garden. The owner grows a range of produce such as kale, potatoes, tomatoes and other salad vegetables. The granitic gravel pathways allow water to permeate into the soil profile; The rainwater storage tanks in the backyard are connected to the house and the collected water is not only used within the home but also to irrigate the garden and fill the billabong; Kale grown in the veggie tanks.

'*Lomandra patens* has a wonderful structure and great architectural potential. It's butterfly-attracting and in the late evenings it also emits a subtle scent. There's lots of green, texture and foliage within this garden. You don't realise you're in suburbia.'

— — — — —

Left: The backyard looking out from the curved timber deck. Aquatic plants in the billabong include *Nymphoides* sp., *Myriophyllum crispatum, Triglochin procerum, Baloskion tetraphyllum* and *Carex fascicularis*. The waterfall can be adjusted to create the desired effect.

Below: A view from the firepit seating area. *Eucalyptus pauciflora* subsp. *debeuzevillei* on the left and *Baloskion tetraphyllum* on the right.

Bottom: This granite boulder was actually positioned to hold a washing basket! It was specially chosen because it was a suitable height. It's small details like this that make a landscape not only aesthetically pleasing but also practical.

A Meditation Garden

A Meditation Garden

The team and I often have to transform a very conventional garden—one that has the standard small garden beds and massive lawns that suffer through the drought—into a more resilient Australian native garden. This project gave me the opportunity to landscape a whole acre within a suburban area, which you don't often get. The aim here was to create a peaceful, relaxing space, as well as a garden that is water efficient and reduces the need for irrigation.

This garden is so different from others in the area. We worked with the environment and the existing trees—*Pinus radiata*, which are evironmental weeds in Victoria. Sometimes in our work the existing trees might have to stay, and before removing any trees we make sure there is no issue with historical significance and that we have the appropriate permits.

This landscape was built in 2006, just as the Victorian drought was worsening and with strict water restrictions in place. In these cirumstances, the owners weren't sure how they could achieve their vision of having water features incorporated into the garden.

We designed two main water features: billabongs at the front and the rear of the residence, crafted with stone. They have been planted with indigenous aquatic plants that help maintain a healthy water quality and create an ecosystem for frogs, dragonflies and water snails.

One of the owners had always wanted a lily pond. She wanted to be able to look out from any window inside the house and see the water lilies. I love water lilies too, but I also like to use indigenous water plants, so it was an enjoyable artistic challenge to blend both together to create a unique result. Water lilies have spectactular flowers, and they are a showy plant—but they go against my philosophy of replicating a natural environment. Water lilies also need to have good depth of water, and they can become dormant from heat stress in our Australian conditions.

The billabongs are designed for viewing from within the house as well as from outside, and this has the effect of bringing the garden into the home. Water flow runs 'inwards', and you can feel how that transforms the entire space into an energising sanctuary. The owners enjoy listening to the waterfalls and watching the birds come in and have a quick swim.

Many years ago this property had been completely stripped and flattened when it was subdivided, and next to no topsoil existed. This is a very common, recurring issue with properties. The topsoil is taken away and you end up with clay. Then you have to buy topsoil later on. However, if you can be involved in the early stages, you can ensure the topsoil is retained. It's got wonderful organic properties.

Taking away the topsoil also creates problems for water drainage. The soil becomes compacted with clay and the soil profile will not be permeable, which is when you get waterlogging.

Suburban properties are usually flattened because it's easier to build on flat land, and this also creates problems when it rains. We wanted to give more

Previous pages
A view of the garden from the meditation room. Stepping stones allow access through the billabong. On either side of the stones we've planted *Lythrum salicaria*. The backdrop of the waterfall has the strong verticals of *Eucalyptus lacrimans*. A stream meanders beneath the boardwalk.

Opposite
The rear billabong, which has been planted with *Triglochin procerum* and *Baloskion tetraphyllum*. The sedimentary rock has been softened with *Acacia cognata* 'Mini Cog'.

Large slabs of stone allow access through the dry creekbed, surrounded by low canopies of vegetation. This view is framed by *Leptospermum* 'Copper Glow'.

natural topography back to the property, so we created mounds and contours, swales and creekbeds. To do this, we brought in locally excavated material that would otherwise have gone to landfill. Altering the contours in this way helped in the management of water flow and stormwater, because water is now redirected into various swales.

Drainage throughout the garden was managed by using local gravel toppings to create permeable paths, which means that water can seep straight through to the ground or overflow off to the garden beds. Permeable paths allow water to percolate through to the soil, giving plants access to this moisture and reducing the need for irrigation.

As with all our gardens, no mains water is used on the garden—all the water in these billabongs is collected as rainwater off the roof. As much stormwater as possible is collected on-site and redirected to various areas for use on the property. If the billabongs did ever dry out, the design ensures they still remain a feature of the garden; the dry creekbed around the front of the house is beautiful both when it's empty or full of overflow from the billabong. The fascinating thing is that the entire landscape will be revived when the rains return—just as it is in a natural ecosystem. Developing these ecosystems is very important. You can see the results in the hordes of butterflies that cluster in this garden, and hear it in the many different bird species that flock here.

We've replumbed all the downpipes and split the roof catchment in half, so that half is directed to the front billabong, and the other half goes to the rear billabong and the rainwater tank. When it rains, the water comes through the downpipes and runs the waterfalls—so both waterfalls flow naturally, based on how much rain is falling on the roof. This is such a beautiful celebration of rain!

Altering the contours of the land has provided the added benefit of creating interesting planting zones for some unique Australian plants, such as *Banksia robur* (swamp banksia) and other dry creekbed species.

Planting has been designed around the brick-veneer house to soften the 1980s architecture. The owners had lived here for twenty-eight years and wanted to distract attention from the exterior of the home. The block was originally covered with at least fifteen pine trees (*Pinus radiata*). So we removed the majority of the trees' upper canopy, resulting in a bold transformation of the space.

As you walk through the garden various pathways lead you in different directions. We've strategically placed stone throughout the garden to guide people through the environment, and provided areas where you can sit and reflect. Every single rock has been hand selected. Apart from drilling a hole in one rock to create a gentle spring, we haven't altered any of them in any way.

Privacy was a big priority for the owners, but no fencing or walling was used. Instead, we created garden 'rooms', screening the property using plants and layering of vegetation rather than building an intrusive, solid wall.

At times I tend to overplant our gardens to allow for plants that could possibly be transplanted later or thinned out. I always like to plant multiple eucalypts, especially small eucalypts, so you get that multi-trunk effect. This gives a sculptural feel. The smaller eucalypts are a great alternative for our urban environments, because people are often concerned about how big gum trees can grow. We've planted some bell-fruited mallee gums (*Eucalyptus preissiana*) as well, which are really quite small and have beautiful flowers.

We also wanted to develop a style of garden that will not date, a garden that will last and evolve with age, and the plants and materials were selected with this in mind. Looking at it now, almost a decade later, it's great to see how the trees have become established over time, and will continue to grow. This habitat looks like it has always been here.

The aim here was to create a very calming space. One of the owners had been quite unwell and this landscape has helped him through the healing process. It is very satisfying to see how these gardens bring joy into people's lives and to experience the healing qualities a landscape can have.

Opposite
Top: A mixture of indigenous plants blends with the white water lilies.

Bottom: Indigenous plantings of *Nymphoides* sp., *Myriophyllum crispatum*, *Baloskion tetraphyllum* and *Marsilea drummondii*.

Epacris longiflora.

Opposite
Clockwise from top left: *Lythrum salicaria*, *Ptilotus* 'Little Joey', *Grevillea sericea*, *Myoporum floribundum*, *Persoonia pinifolia*, *Ammobium alatum*, *Anigozanthos flavidus* 'Bush Gold', *Acacia glaucoptera*. Centre: *Anigozanthos flavidus* 'Big Red'.

Following pages
Eucalyptus pauciflora has beautiful trunk formations when planted in a group. The plants in this garden have created their own pathway by growing into the gravel and softening the edges between the path and garden.

Following pages

Left: Stepping stones through a
sea of purple *Lythrum salicaria*.

Right: Detail of *Anigozanthos
flavidus* 'Big Red' and *Ammobium
alatum*.

The Fern Garden

The Fern Garden

The aim for this property in suburban Melbourne was to create an environment for the whole family to interact with, to play in and to grow veggies in. But the unusual element of this landscape was that the owner, Mirini, was a fern enthusiast, and our goal was to create a framework for her so that she could fulfil her dream of having a fernery in her very own backyard.

The first time we visited the site it was just a dust bowl—and we wanted to build a thriving fernery! It sounded crazy. It was a hard environment to work with. It had clay soil and building rubble everywhere, and our challenge was to transform it into a lush environment. The owner had an architecturally designed shade structure that allowed a certain amount of light to come through for the ferns, and which also acted to screen off the new subdivision next door.

Standing in the garden now, you would not know you were in the suburbs. But these suburbs weren't always like this. We used to have such beautiful, delicate ecosystems everywhere, and it's important to try to build them back where we can. A landscape such as this one is also helping to counteract the urban 'heat island' effect, where we have too much concrete in our urban environments, where everything absorbs heat—and there's no relief.

As you enter the fernery, you walk along some stone steps and have to lift a fern to pass under it. So immediately you're engaging in a tactile and sensory way with the environment. There are over seventy different species of fern in this garden. Ferns need more water than most plants, and the fernery is irrigated and sustained by the stormwater from the property. All the roof water is collected and stored in tanks under the house, which were cleverly installed when the house was being built. It's a good way of utilising the space under the house instead of taking up room in the garden. This isn't always possible, as each property has constraints.

Mirini has created a wonderful collection of specimens in her fernery. Spontaneous ferns have grown there naturally. Spores are transported by the wind, and when they land on a moist spot, with the right conditions, a new fern will grow.

It's such a peaceful space to potter around in. Mirini often goes into the fernery and eats lunch seated on the coolness of the step.

In the front section we've created an ephemeral dry creekbed. When it rains the creekbed fills up, and because it's semi-permeable, it absorbs water; this slowly percolates throughout the soil, slowing the stormwater down. This process also traps silt.

The owners were passionate about conserving electricity and water. On average over the year they generate more electricity than they use. They have enough solar panels to run the house, and the tank water is connected to the toilets and washing machine, so they're really reducing their energy and water footprint. They've also planted a thriving veggie patch and a lawn for the kids to play on.

The owner's love of ferns has now taken her on a journey into further horticultural studies: this garden has inspired her. This is how a garden can become a life passion.

Previous pages
The view from the house is breathtaking, looking out onto a lush fernery. Slabs of stone are used to bridge the little creeks that run through this fernery.

Opposite
Delicate rock placement helps to channel and redirect water as it moves down the natural slope of the property.

Pteris vittata. A new growth unwinding—a truly remarkable sight.

Opposite
Clockwise from top left: Layering of various ferns; Intricate placement of rocks and foliage provides a striking contrast; The light reflecting off the water creates a lovely rippling effect; *Selaginella kraussiana* growing around the rocks.

'As you enter the fernery, you walk along some stone steps and have to lift a fern to pass under it. So immediately you're engaging in a tactile and sensory way with the environment. There are over seventy different species of fern in this garden.'

Clockwise from top left:
Microsorum pustulatum subsp.
pustulatum; *Dicksonia antarctica*;
Blechnum moorei; *Dicksonia
antarctica*; *Blechnum moorei*;
Dicksonia antarctica; *Dicksonia
antarctica*. Centre: *Microsorum
pustulatum* subsp. *howense*.

Opposite
Adiantum raddianum.

Lubra Bend

Lubra Bend

This beautiful 300 acre (121 hectare) property has a rich history. It's situated on a bend in the Yarra River and was named Lubra Bend in the 1860s by newspaper proprietor David Syme: 'lubra' was the term by which colonial settlers referred to the nursing Aboriginal women who camped here. The house was designed by renowned Australian architect Guilford Bell in 1959 for local member of parliament Russell Stokes and his wife, Margaret.

The current owner, Rosemary Simpson, moved here in 2000 and wanted to honour the property's significant history by bringing it up to a very high standard. She felt like the custodian of the property, and wanted to inspire her family and future generations. Rosemary and I share a passion for how important sustainable landscapes are in this extremely arid country.

Our aim was to create a dry garden—one that would never need watering. Rosemary has a great appreciation for natural stone and landscapes, inspired by memories of her time spent living in the Strathbogies, Victoria, where she fell in love with granite.

Rosemary was committed to creating the garden in three stages: the first stage involved the upper pools, the second stage involved the cascade and wetlands, and the third stage involved the habitat corridor. Although the build took ten months in total, the completion of the project spanned a few years. It's a large historical property, and the scale and the size of what we were proposing could potentially have been very intimidating and disruptive. I thought it was a good idea to allow the garden some time to grow before going on to the next stage.

Part of the brief was that we had to blend our design into the existing vegetation and landscape. Rosemary wanted to build a landscape that would work *with* the environment, not against it.

This is a working country property, not a highly managed, manicured garden. The farm is the main area that requires most of the owner's time, and the garden is secondary. It was important that the landscape connected beautifully to the other aspects of the property: the swimming pool, garden, croquet lawn and kitchen garden.

The top dry garden was constructed during the driest period ever experienced in the region. The entry to Lubra Bend was originally a barren paddock, which had made establishing plant growth difficult. However, on the positive side, a sixty-year-old cypress hedge, planted by the previous owner, offered a very effective wind break. This allowed us to create a wonderful microclimate in a location that would otherwise have been too windy and exposed—without the wind break it simply would not have been a peaceful space. The protection the cypress hedge gave enabled us to enhance what the previous owner had started and take it to another level.

Because it's such a large area, about 5 acres (2 hectares), we had to design something quite dramatic, which worked with the environment. We couldn't use little pebbles or other materials that would look out of place. So as you drive in, one

Previous pages
The early morning view through the remnant *Eucalyptus yarraensis*. It's hard to believe this area was once a tennis court.

Opposite
There is a range of indigenous aquatic plants here, including *Leptospermum* 'Copper Glow'. The owner also introduced *Nelumbo nucifera* (lotus). The stepping stones allow you to walk across the pool.

Above: Stepping stones have been carefully selected to be consistent in size and laid level to make it easy to walk across the pool. Planting pockets have been created between the rocks.

Right: View of the public entrance to the garden through a small clipped hole in the cypress hedge.

Opposite
Eucalyptus lacrimans (weeping snow gum).

of the first things you see is this incredible 30 tonne piece of granite. We've buried the rock slightly, but not too much, because we didn't want to lose the magnitude of the rock.

Originally the driveway ran straight up against the cypress hedge, but we've changed it by redirecting it so that it's now more like an S-bend, to slow you down and create more of an experience as you enter the property. We've used a granitic base topping on the driveway. The camber, or fall, of the driveway is now directed towards the upper and lower pools.

Rosemary had planned to undertake major earth works to relocate her power supply underground, as opposed to having power poles, so we scheduled that into our works. The contour of the landscape was raised and excavated in various areas. There was no imported soil used; everything was reused from the site. We have used a massive number of ground covers, including *Banksia blechnifolia*, *Acacia pravissima* and *Banksia petiolaris*.

Guests are invited to enter the property via a small, inconspicuous opening— like a tunnel way—through the cypress hedge. Coming through the cypress hedge, there is a beautiful view that looks out to the upper pool, and to the *Eucalyptus yarraensis*, a remarkable species of eucalypt that is indigenous to the Yarra Glen area.

Water is extremely precious in this country, and Rosemary understands this. The garden isn't irrigated; no mains water is used within the landscape. We've built two pools here. Overflow from the upper pool flows into the lower pool by way of a beautiful spillway, and then the overflow from the lower pool connects up at the cascade, which makes its way down to the lower wetland. The driveway run-off and the roof water are sent to these pools and used to sustain them. During a downpour, the dry creekbed has the potential to come alive like a rapid.

There's a whole range of aquatic plants throughout the pools, including *Leptospermum* 'Copper Glow' on the edge of the upper pool. Rosemary has also introduced lotuses, which are just stunning.

You can hear the frogs as you walk through the landscape: there are seven different species here at different times of the year.

Stepping stones are one of our signature design elements. They meander across the pool—they feel so solid underfoot, and yet you feel like you're walking on the water. Stepping stones connect people back to the landscape; they are one of those tactile experiences I think you need to have within a landscape. My favourite piece of stone is what I describe as 'the change of angle stone', more of a triangle shape, which allows you to change the angle of a path. It's not a straight line, it's a bend. The natural beauty that's occurred between these stepping stones, the way the plants have just settled in between them, is something we drew on for inspiration to replicate at Chelsea. It makes them look like they've been there for a long time.

Stone deserves respect. It needs to be placed with consideration, because it's there for life. The plants might change and evolve, but these rocks and this experience will be here for a very long time.

I find it incredibly exciting to discover new ways of creating amazing vistas. And sometimes it can take more than ten years before a view really starts to show itself. If you walk around the roundabout rock you get a glimpse of the waterfall at certain points. We planned this so that not everything is revealed straight away, it's revealed in certain strategic stages. There's an element of surprise within the landscape.

The crucible rock was a main feature. It's located at the bottom of the driveway, near the house, and is such a sculptural component—it works so well in the large space and the grand scale we had to design with. The piece of stone also has the ability to capture its own water, providing a very shallow pool for finches and other small birds to use as a birdbath.

Our second stage of building was the creation of the cascade and wetlands. Originally this area was an old disused tennis court, overgrown with blackberries and wisteria. I purposely left one post of the tennis court fence there to remind people how we've transformed the space.

During the Black Saturday events of January 2009 the fire came up and stopped at these wetlands. Rosemary called me the day after and told me how grateful she was that we'd built the wetlands, which had stopped the spread of the fire up the valley to the residence. A few banksias were affected, the lawn was scorched, they lost all their fences and the paddocks were burned. But these wetlands saved the homestead.

Rosemary didn't want a formal structured pathway that went down to the wetlands, she wanted visitors to take their own journey, which I think is wonderful.

The final stage of our build was 180 metres of work that created a habitat corridor to connect the wetlands of Lubra Bend with the Yarra River, so that animals would be able to move up and down between the two habitats. Originally the water went from the wetlands, across the paddock, to the Yarra River. We wanted to slow the water down and have it meandering through a creekbed, which was planted with indigenous aquatic plants. This helped create a great environment, linked the water and connected the design. It also helped bring the paddock alive.

It's a unique experience to work on such a historic property and to design on such a grand scale. And it's crucial on a project like this to be respectful of the historical significance of this kind of property. The original owners had a vision, and Rosemary had a vision—and she's taken it to an exciting level. You're the custodian of your land, no matter how small or grand it is, and while it's in your possession it's up to you and your family to apply the best environmental input to help improve it for future generations.

Rosemary says the garden keeps her inspired and motivated. She gets up early each day and goes out into it, to see what's occurred as well as to harvest produce. A landscape can help keep your mind active and stimulated, and energise you on a daily basis.

This 30 tonne roundabout rock is framed by the magnificent *Eucalyptus yarraensis* in the distance.

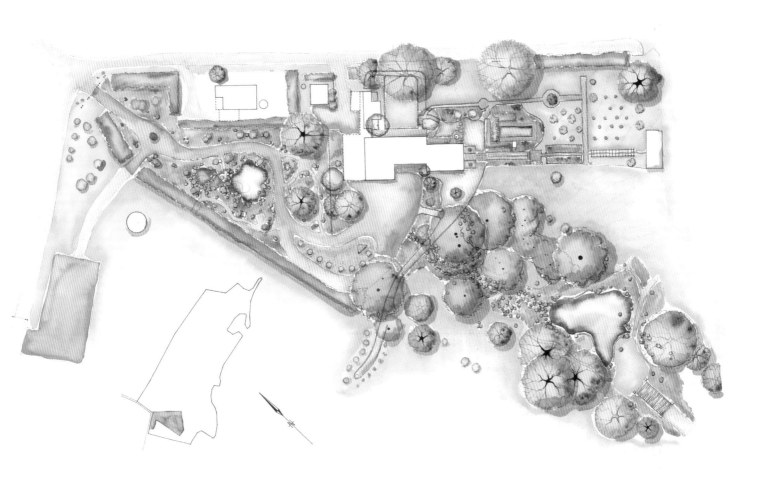

Clockwise from top right: Watercolour plan of the landscape design; The snaking pathway takes the explorer on a journey through the garden; The spillway from the upper pool to the lower pool; The curving driveway; Weddings are now held on this lawn, which used to be a tennis court; The crucible rock— a 35 tonne rock that is not only a beautiful sculpture but also acts as a natural birdbath.

Eucalyptus yarraensis sit either side of the cascade lined with bronze granite to retain the gradient down to the wetland.

Following pages
Left: The wetland. A curved bluestone wall creates the vantage point.

Right: Early morning light—spider webs attach to the tips of *Juncus holoschoenus*.

'Part of the brief was that we had to blend our design into the existing vegetation and landscape. Rosemary wanted to build a landscape that would work *with* the environment, not against it.'

— — — — —

Left: The perfect sunrise vantage point of Lubra Bend—the Yarra Valley. The bridge is made from reclaimed railway sleepers. To the right, *Fraxinus angustifolia* subsp. *oxycarpa*.

Below: Pear sculpture by George Baldessin.

Bottom: The wetland in the early morning.

A Memorial Garden

A Memorial Garden

This garden holds special meaning for me. It shows how a garden has the power to help heal the soul. The owner, Maria, was mourning the loss of her husband, Harry, and she wanted to create a garden in memory of him. Creating a memorial garden dedicated to someone is such a beautiful way to leave a legacy and to honour someone's life. Rarely do we have the opportunity to work on a project that has so much emotion behind it. This is my favourite small garden—Harry's Garden.

It was really moving going to meet Maria for the first time. She had Handel's *Water Music* playing in the background. As I listened to the melodies and the stories she told me of Harry, I came understand how important this garden was.

Originally, there was a caravan and a car parked in the front garden, so I had to see past those. You have to imagine what could be. I had to see the beauty that was hidden.

The complexity in this front yard is extraordinary. It's a small space, 8 metres by 2.5 metres—just the width of a caravan—so there were logistical challenges around getting access to the space and the shared driveway.

In some ways, it's easier to appreciate a small garden like this because it allows you to focus on the details. Everywhere you look there's interest, from the intricate rock placement to the way the water snails move across the surface of the billabong, assisting in keeping the system clean. This is a garden best enjoyed in solitude.

The inspiration for the garden came from camping trips that Maria had taken with Harry to Mount Buangor in Victoria. She wanted us to mimic the smell of the earth and the water—that really organic scent you find out in nature. She came up to my place in Olinda and loved the smell of our billabongs and wanted to re-create them in her own garden. In order to do that the team and I have constructed areas of moving water: when the water splashes, it disperses and releases its earthy odour.

You can take different pathways to the front door and to the private sitting area within the garden. As a microclimate, this gets quite hot; it has a west-facing aspect, so the afternoon sun hits the sitting area. Two bubbling rocks, which are adjustable, assist in cooling the space. It's always tricky getting the music of running water right—it could just be a trickle, or more of a cascade. We always build our waterfalls so they are adjustable, and we can alter them to get the right flow of water for each landscape.

Around the water we've used a range of different stones to create the delicate rock work. These stepping stones across the billabong give you the feeling of walking on water before you arrive at the seating area, a place for reflection and meditation. The LED night lighting transforms the landscape in the evenings … It comes alive and has its own magic.

The rocks are the bones of the landscape, but this also meant that at the completion of the project, before the plants became fully established, it looked very rocky and nude. However, the plants will flourish in the nooks and

Previous pages
The beautiful reclaimed wharf timbers add a rustic character to this urban garden while at the same time reusing a valuable resource.

Opposite
These stepping stones take you on a journey to the front door. Take either the direct route or linger on the longer path, past the bubbling rock.

A Memorial Garden

crannies; they will grow and soften the landscape, and so the memorial garden will evolve with time.

Even in a small space like this one we've built infrastructure underground to slow down and redirect stormwater. The waterhole is a key feature. We wanted to get the water level of the billabong up quite high so it could be seen from the verandah and the residence. It is planted with one of my favourite water plants, a water ribbon called *Triglochin*.

For the fence we used recycled wharf pylon offcuts, which have a personal connection for Maria. When we were sourcing timber for this project, our site manager, Michael, discovered the pylons from the old Appleton Docks in Melbourne. Harry used to work there! Maria couldn't believe it. You can see the shells of crustaceans still clinging to them. There are little cut-outs in the fence, so that the gas and water meters can be read from the street.

Maria recently told me that her father, a retired stonemason—who had sat in the garden for many hours during the last few days of his life—kept shaking his head and saying, 'I still can't believe how they got these rocks in!' She said that sitting in the garden each day had kept his mind active and curious as he enjoyed the peaceful surrounds.

Maria says she can feel Harry's spirit within the garden. She believes her connection to the memorial garden has helped her heal more than she ever expected.

Clockwise from top left: Sit by the billabong and listen to the delicate sounds of falling water and the croaking of frogs, and watch the birds and insects play in the small space of this urban front garden; The view from the bench seat where the owner's father spent his last days marvelling at the beauty of the garden; A private gate into the garden; Detail of *Doodia aspera*.

'Originally, there was a caravan and a car parked in the front garden, so I had to see past those. You have to imagine what could be. I had to see the beauty that was hidden.'

Detailed rock placement is used
to disguise any artificial aspects
of the billabong.

Opposite
Top: Detail of the reclaimed
timber gate.

Bottom: The mix of sizes and
colours of stone.

The vertical lines of the *Baloskion tetraphyllum* and the flower spikes of *Xerochrysum palustre* provide a dramatic structural contrast against the rocky waterfall.

Viola hederacea growing in the
moist shelter of the waterfall.

Opposite
Even a small waterfall can
enchant with its gentle sounds.

Using ageing logs adds a distinct character and creates a habitat for insects and lizards.

Opposite
As you enter the garden through the gate, you are instantly immersed in the energy of the landscape.

The Birthday Garden

The Birthday Garden

When Rebecca and Craig first moved into this property, they hardly ever went into the garden. The previous owners had been an elderly retired couple who had built a very formal courtyard, with brick walls, hedges and neat garden beds. Rebecca and Craig didn't want to have a rose garden like every other house on the street.

Being a busy, young working family, they didn't have much time to tend to the garden. They'd just been through the drought, and the turf and plants had suffered, resulting in big, gaping voids in the garden beds. The original garden had a small, metre-square fish pond; while they wanted to keep a water feature of some sort, Craig was interested in water sustainability and liked the idea of something that would be useful beyond simply aesthetic value. This garden was a gift Craig and Rebecca gave to each other for their fortieth birthdays.

The aim with this project was to build a low-maintenance, water-efficient landscape, and to encourage their two young children to get out into the garden more.

We installed a 4000 litre rainwater tank in the garage. The owners didn't want it taking up space in their backyard. The water collected in the tank is used to water the garden as well as to fill the billabong, if required. It's amazing to realise how much water was going to waste before, and to see how much Rebecca and Craig can collect now just by incorporating an integrated water cycle management system into their garden.

Rebecca wanted to try growing her own veggies and herbs. She'd never had a veggie patch before, and since she and her family lead very busy lives, my advice was to start with something small and simple instead of jumping in and having a massive vegetable garden. Once she'd got the knack of it, she could build from there. So we've used three disused wine barrels and planted just a few herbs, such as basil, parsley and thyme. This is a simple way to start developing your green thumb.

Every day the owners come through the garage door into the garden and walk along the meandering path, which slows them down and gives them a chance to enjoy the space. Craig has a high-pressure job, and to de-stress now he just walks out into the garden. Through just pottering around, pulling out a weed here or there, he's discovered it's a great way to relax and connect with the environment. You get the same feeling just sitting in the garden and listening to the sound of the water. The owners like watching the birds bathing in the billabong, dipping in and out, and skipping into and under the water.

This landscape shows how a space can be adapted and modelled to fit a busy lifestyle. It's a xeriscape landscape approach—a dry garden that doesn't require watering due to appropriate plant selection. The only thing that requires irrigation is the small patch of lawn and the vegetables and herbs.

This garden shows just how beautiful our plant palette is in Australia. We have an incredible patchwork of colours—it's not just bottlebrush and tea trees. There are so many shades of yellow, red and purple in this garden. We used

— — — —

'The owners like watching the birds bathing in the billabong, dipping in and out, and skipping into and under the water.'

— — — —

Previous pages
A courtyard that was previously hot and uninviting is now a space where the family can reconnect and re-energise.

Opposite
Even in a small space, a billabong can cool the area and create a habitat for frogs, lizards, birds, butterflies and other insects.

paper daisies, kangaroo paws and banksias to introduce more colour. This is something the owners requested, and it is easily achievable, even in a suburban backyard.

The brick wall creates a challenging environment in winter months, limiting the amount of sunlight. We had to make sure we used shade-tolerant plants.

An old plinth was relocated to become a seat. We placed it near the billabong, and it's now a great spot to sit, relax and view the garden, with the sound of the billabong behind you. When I first visit a garden, I look at what else is there and what can potentially be reused before the property is stripped. We also reused all the soil. We didn't let any leave the site.

The front of the house is a very traditional landscape. The owners are now planning to transform it so that it connects with the back garden.

I find it strange that Australians often ignore what we have. We want an English cottage garden, or a bit of French provincial, some Tuscan, or some Zen. Anything but what we already have! We should be aiming to use what works well with our environment—native and indigenous plants—as Rebecca and Craig have done in their garden.

Dappled light in the late afternoon highlights the colours of the flowers. All the paths are permeable, allowing water to infiltrate the ground.

Marsilea drummondii and
Myriophyllum crispatum absorb
nutrients from the water, helping
to keep it clean and crystal clear.

Opposite
Dichondra repens finding its
own path between the rocks and
water.

'This garden shows just how beautiful our plant palette is in Australia. We have an incredible patchwork of colours—it's not just bottlebrush and tea trees. There are so many shades of yellow, red and purple in this garden. We used paper daisies, kangaroo paws and banksias to introduce more colour.'

— — — — — —

Left: The cheerful yellow of *Xerochrysum bracteatum* 'Cockatoo' brightens this courtyard for many months and is a great cut flower.

Below: Detail of *Anigozanthos flavidus* 'Big Red'. Contrasting forms and colours are imperative in good planting design.

Bottom: The rock seat provides a tranquil place to relax among the colours and scents of the garden. Plants include *Chrysocephalum apiculatum*, *Xerochrysum bracteatum* 'Cockatoo' and *Anigozanthos flavidus* 'Big Red'.

The Evolving Garden

The Evolving Garden

I often describe landscape design as like painting on a canvas, and this property is an example of what I mean by that. When the sliding doors of the living space are opened up to the outside, you get a spectacular view of the framed landscape. This garden has all the depth of a painting; the carefully positioned bronze granite rock forms and curved ribbon of 270 'Big Red' kangaroo paws draw the eye down into it and create a relaxing environment that extends back into the home.

Although the architecture of the house is very modern, the natural colours work in seamlessly with the landscape.

The owner has a love of the earth—her background is in geography—but she's been unable to travel as much as she used to. Her son has autism, and her dream was to create a peaceful landscape at home that gave a sense of being in another place, and encouraged discovery and exploration. The owner describes the landscape as being an opportunity to travel with her mind. It's a garden of experiences.

The garden is for the family, to energise and inspire them, and we went through multiple revisions to get the project right for them. There are sweeping vistas that you can view from many different vantage points, but when you look closer you notice the smaller details: the plantings between the rocks, and an enormous variety of colours and textures.

This garden is like an urban farm. There are so many different sorts of fruits and vegetables, from beans, radishes and beetroot, to citrus, strawberries and guava. The beautiful sensory herb garden contains several types of mint and basil, as well as rosemary, lemongrass, elderflower, lemon verbena and stevia. Just taking a short stroll through this landscape will stimulate your senses.

The owner asked that the majority of plants be edible. She has planted nasturtiums, calendula, violas and carnations, all of which can be used in salads or baking.

The owner also wanted a low-maintenance garden, and didn't want to spend time mowing lawns. She wanted to use her available water to sustain the produce and top up the pool.

It's a young garden, only twelve months old as I write, and it's still evolving. The landscape and the house were constructed simultaneously and it was a really complicated build in terms of project management. We had to work with the builder—we only had access at certain times to implement certain stages of work. There were many different stages involved, based on access. This landscape took approximately five months to build.

When we were in the early phase of the project, the family came to visit my garden in Olinda and swam in our old style of billabong, which at that time had no filtration system at all—you're basically swimming in a natural wetland system. But they enjoyed it, and the experience inspired them to create a natural pool of their own. You can actually make the water clean without using chemicals.

Previous pages
The rock wall creates an infinity edge for this natural pool. *Eleocharis sphacelata* in the filtration zone aids in water purification by taking up excess nutrients from the water. *Carpobrotus rossii* provides a bushfood snack.

Opposite
The expanse of glass allows unobstructed views of the landscape and also reflects it from the outside, creating a stunning connection between the house and the garden. The shallow beach has been designed for children to play in.

The billabong is a natural chemical-free swimming pool that has been designed to fluctuate. The pool here is one of the first we designed with an infinity edge. The owner wanted this feature, and we built it out of intricate stonework, which was quite time consuming and labour intensive. The stonemasons have done a meticulous job in creating the infinity edge wall within 1–2 millimetres in relation to the water level. The water runs off the edge to a small pond, that run-off goes back into the pool, and this is all connected to their rainwater tank.

The waterfall has been designed so that it faces the living space. It's adjustable, which means the water can be kept to just a trickle, and there's lighting, so it can be viewed at night.

Stormwater is captured and stored in a 40,000 litre tank, which means the family can use this, rather than their mains water, for irrigation. The garden also features a hot spring, which adds another relaxing element to this landscape.

One of the owners saw our winning garden at the Melbourne International Flower and Garden Show in 2009. She came back multiple times with her family to walk through and experience the landscape. The curved decking was one of the features in our show concept—it's one of our signatures. We created a curved deck for this garden, as well as a boardwalk that takes you across to the back of the area. It provides great access to the rest of the garden. The boardwalk also hides the skimmer.

We designed the pond that sits in the alcove because the owners wanted something very special in that space. This area is like a painting. We placed a large rock next to the pond where you can sit, and at certain times of the day you can experience this lovely play of light against the building, the windows and the water. The pond features a bubbling rock that's been carved out and honed. As I've said before, it's so important to get the sound of moving, flowing water right. It takes fine-tuning.

The owners have created a peaceful, relaxing environment that gently defuses stress. Strolling through or working in the garden is cathartic and relaxing.

Produce is an important element in this garden. Fragrant herbs are within easy reach and mingle beautifully with native plants surrounding the pool.

Top: Crystal-clear water lets you see the pebble filtration zone. Stepping stones take you on an alternative journey to the boardwalk.

Bottom: *Poa labillardieri* frames the beautifully handcrafted stonemasonry work of the hot spring.

Opposite
Top: The soft breeze creates mesmerising ripples on the water.

Bottom: There is an art to creating a beautiful stone wall. Here the stone wall has been built to create an infinity edge, allowing the water to flow gently over it into the filtration zone.

Plants mix and mingle between
the rocks, providing a soft
contrast against the hard stone.
Species include *Tagetes patula*,
Hardenbergia violacea and
Poa labillardieri.

Agastache foeniculum grows well with the additional moisture from the waterfall spray.

Opposite
Top: The borrowed landscape makes this garden appear bigger than it is. The natural pool provides a unique swimming experience.

Bottom: *Poa labillardieri* provides a strong structural contrast to the horizontal lines of the rock steps and the low-growing forms of *Tagetes patula* and *Dianthus* sp.

'The pond has a bubbling rock that's been honed out. This area is like a painting. We placed a large rock next to the pond where you can sit, and at certain times of the day you get this lovely play of light against the building, the windows and the water.'

— — — — —

Left: A tranquil billabong in this small courtyard can be viewed from various rooms and helps cool the house through natural, evaporative cooling.

Below: We searched long and hard to find the perfect granite boulder to create this beautiful bubbling rock.

Bottom: *Dichondra repens* creeping through the rocks.

The Turtle Habitat

The Turtle Habitat

One of the owners of this garden, Graham, is a passionate turtle conservationist, and his wife, Jill, has supported his mission all the way. We wanted this to be not only a refuge for the terrestrial turtles he has rescued, but also a complete urban habitat where turtles could continue to live, reproduce and thrive.

This project was a great challenge. You don't often go to work and get asked to create a turtle habitat! There were a few considerations specific to turtle habitats that we had to keep in mind when designing this landscape. First, turtles can dig, so we had to contain the whole garden so they wouldn't be able to burrow under the house or the fence and get under the neighbours' footings. There also needed to be good depth of water in the billabong, and areas that allowed the turtles to get in and out easily. Shelter and protection were also really important, and we've achieved this through the use of stones and logs. Softer, flat rocks provide sunbaking surfaces.

The brief was to create a gentle environment for the turtles. We worked with flat sheets of dark mudstone, which allowed us to 'spread the water out', so that it flowed into the billabong as a soft trickle. The turtles have taken well to this new environment. There are more than ten turtles in the billabong, along with fish and yabbies. Indigenous aquatic plant species help to keep the water clean, while also providing habitat. We've tried to mimic a healthy natural environment in the same way a good zoo enclosure would, by replicating a natural system.

It's a very young garden, but you can see already how it's starting to flourish. The owners wanted a landscape that would always be in flower, to attract birds and butterflies, and while more birds will come later on when the trees are more established, the butterflies have already arrived. This relatively new garden is destined to evolve even more as it becomes more established.

There wasn't a lot here beforehand. We had to work around the existing banksias and incorporate a lot of shade-providing plants. Graham and Jill live adjacent to a local park and the vision was to create a backyard that connected to the surrounding environment. We used a combination of Australian natives and indigenous plants.

The owners collect 15,000 litres of water off their property, and it's part of the integrated water cycle management system. When the billabong overflows, any seed, root matter or rhizome that's present in the water can be passed into the stormwater as well. This goes into our local waterways, so we're helping to seed back into the system, helping to heal our waterways. These sorts of plants exist everywhere around the world. You just need to do some research to find out which indigenous plants exist in your waterways, and then work with them.

Permeable gravel paths allow water to percolate through the soil instead of leaving it to just run off a hard surface. The only design flaw in selecting this material is that you will need a good transition between the surface of the path and the house—maybe slabs of stone or decking—to allow you to remove the gravel from your feet and your shoes before you go inside.

— — — —

'There are more than ten turtles in the billabong, along with fish and yabbies. Indigenous aquatic plants help to keep the water clean and healthy.'

— — — —

Previous pages
This lush green garden creates a haven for the occupants, both human and reptile, as the owner rescues and breeds native turtles.

Opposite
Clockwise from top left: One of the rescued turtles; This strategically placed piece of wood provides a ramp for the turtles to get in and out of the billabong; Large rocks provide shelter for the turtles; The turtle billabong is surrounded by shade-providing plants.

Little bush tracks allow for exploration of this lovely backyard—where humans and turtles live in harmony.

The paths blend in with the surrounding garden beds. We like to have certain plants on the edges of the pathways so it looks like they're just emerging; this assists in softening the look as well.

A practical folding clothesline is positioned on the west fence, to make the most of the sun hitting the area, as well as to save space and for reasons of functionality and access to the laundry. A design trick I've applied a few times in my projects is planting some lavender near the clothesline, hopefully allowing the scent to infuse your clothes. Just watch out for bees getting too up close and personal!

The owners have two teenagers, so they also wanted an outdoor entertaining area for parties and family get-togethers. This is a great place to entertain. The owners regularly have company, and they like to sit out on the rocks by the billabong and enjoy the fire. We've created an environment where the whole family wants to hang out and be surrounded by this turtle habitat.

When you have a nearby park, why not try to flow that right into your backyard, making it a borrowed landscape? We added more bird-attracting plants, and this also created a habitat for butterflies and other insects. This garden, like most of our landscapes, doesn't have mosquitoes.

My dream is for everyone to have backyards like this, connected to communities and neighbourhoods.

Detail of the waterfall in the
billabong. Flat sheets of dark slate
were used to slow down the water
for the turtles.

Opposite
Top: The deep dark waters of this
billabong provide shelter and
protection and a source of food
for the turtle inhabitants.

Bottom: The family firepit.

Clockwise from top left: *Bulbine bulbosa; Banksia repens; Baloskion tetraphyllum; Acacia leprosa* 'Scarlet Blaze'; *Ficinia nodosa; Viola hederacea; Cyathea australis.*
Centre: *Dampiera stricta* 'Glasshouse Glory'.

Opposite
Chrysocephalum apiculatum.

Viola hederacea helps soften this large rock.

Opposite
The gravel path provides a permeable surface for water to infiltrate the soil. The firepit is a gathering space for the family.

The Bushwalking Garden

The Bushwalking Garden

The owners of this property, which sits on 3.5 acres (1.4 hectares), are passionate bushwalkers. Kylie and Michael both have a love of the outdoors, and an appreciation of the natural beauty of Australia, and this is where the inspiration for the garden came from. This garden has also been created for their children. With three active boys, they definitely needed space. So we've designed a landscape that will work for them as they grow. There is a veggie patch, sandpits, tracks around the whole property they can ride their bikes on, and bodies of water that are safe and secure all the time. There's also a sensory children's garden.

The new residence required quite significant retaining: a minimum of 1.5 metres in some areas. But the owners didn't want to look out at an ugly sleeper retaining wall; they wanted something beautiful. So instead of having a wall made out of a combination of steel H-section and sleepers—which would probably need to be replaced within fifteen to twenty years' time anyway—we decided to design a retaining wall that was permanent, that did not need to be replaced, that created interest and was beautiful, and that formed a habitat for lizards and other animals. The obvious choice was rock, of course!

I love working with rock because it's a permanent resource that will last hundreds of thousands of years. It also allows easy flow of water through the site, as well as through the gaps and cracks in the wall, where plants can grow. It's not a barrier that's suppressing the water, it has water moving through it.

Travelling around the world I've been really privileged to see a range of different landscapes that use rock. I've witnessed how remarkable the Japanese are at placing stepping stones (I'm inspired by the Japanese in terms of rock design), and I've had the opportunity to hike the four-day Inca trail to Machu Picchu in the Andes, with its incredible dry-stone walling. But Australia has Uluru, the Kimberleys and Kakadu. We have Wilsons Promontory, the Grampians, the Blue Mountains, Litchfield National Park and the Flinders Ranges. We've got such amazing natural rock formations.

Rock is a material that doesn't date. It is also a resource we have available: it isn't manufactured, it has basically gone through just the one process of getting it out of the ground. Think of the energy that goes into making a single concrete block, or a piece of steel—an incredible amount. I also think rock has so much character. The wall in this garden is a celebration of stone.

The way I describe our rock-placement principle is: randomality! It's my favourite word. My little boy taught it to me. He brought in a handful of pebbles from the garden one day and dropped them onto our floorboards and it created a great pattern. I apply those same principles in our designs.

I've always admired the Australian garden designer Edna Walling. She used to decide where to plant by throwing potatoes onto a patch of ground, and then she would plant the seeds where the potatoes landed. A similar technique can be used with rocks. In my projects I use many different sizes, textures and shapes, from huge boulders right down to very small rocks. We study each one so we can place the rocks in a way that closely reflects how they would occur in

Previous pages
Morning by the billabong
overlooking the Yarra Valley.

Opposite
Parthenocissus quinquefolia
(also known as Virginia creeper)
softens the hard lines of
the house.

nature. It's important to use rocks of different sizes in a landscape. Small rocks can balance, soften and connect with bigger rocks. They enhance one another.

At times, when we're creating an environment and placing stone, the rocks we use need to serve a functional purpose. Some are used for waterfalls, to help move water a certain way; some are there to allow people to get up close and experience being right within nature; others are necessary for creating structural retaining walls. After this garden's wall was built, Kylie and Michael said it reminded them how much they loved rock. The kids also love jumping off these rocks and playing on them.

A recent stage of works involved the upgrade of an old leaking dam in order to turn it into a large billabong. We built a series of stepping stones that guide you through shallow areas to the cascading waterfall, which has been strategically positioned so you can view it as you drive through the gates of the property, and from the study, the kitchen sink and the master bedroom. I took inspiration from the billabongs that occur naturally along the Yarra Flats, a local feature of the area's landscape.

Our design also incorporates a series of staircases that meander through the property. The staircases allow ease of access to the landscape, and each stairway we design has a 170 millimetre rise. I want anyone to be able to walk up and down it comfortably.

When it came to water management, fire protection was very much on Kylie and Michael's minds. In fire-prone areas, it's important to have as much available water as possible. We installed water tanks under the grass-tree garden that can hold up to 100,000 litres.

One of our design principles in fire-prone areas is to avoid having organic mulches next to the residence. So what we use instead is an inorganic, non-combustible mulch, such as a stone aggregate.

The owners always wanted to grow their own produce. We put veggie boxes close to the house so that the owners see them daily. Kylie and Michael had originally planned a tennis court, but now this area has an orchard, veggie patch, cubby house, compost facility, playground and bike track.

The landscape blends in well with the contours of the Yarra Valley. When I work on a project I spend a lot of time within the landscape observing the contours and the terrain—then I see how I can use these as design drivers.

At the time I became involved in the project, the original old house had burned down and the garden was full of weedy species. But we had lovely vistas to work with.The owners have stunning aspects from different viewlines of the new house, so when they walk up their stairs they can just stop for a moment and look out into their landscape.

The garden gets everyone in the family outside more, which is exactly what the owners wanted. That's what more people need to do. Kylie, Michael and their children spend weekends exploring the garden.

Opposite
Clockwise from top left: The rocky gorge; The children's sensory garden, where plant species include *Pimelea nivea, Eucalyptus pauciflora, Lomandra confertifolia* subsp. *rubiginosa* 'Seascape', and *Scaevola aemula* 'Mauve Clusters'; The tyre swing; Perfectly positioned stone steps softened by *Dianella* 'Little Jess'.

The rocky waterfall.

Opposite
Sunrise makes the chardonnay
vines glow golden. Two sets of
stepping stones take you to a
central spot, providing a lovely
vantage point for viewing the
waterfall.

Top: The dry creek connects the house to the larger billabong. Climbers like this Virginia creeper help to cool a building and provide shade for a refreshing space to sit on a summer's day.

Bottom: The dramatic slabs of granite are softened by the planting, which includes *Dianella* 'Little Jess' and *Scaevola aemula* 'Mauve Clusters'.

Opposite
Top: The silver of the beautiful untreated timber pergola blends perfectly with the rocks and waves of green plants such as *Banksia integrifolia* 'Roller Coaster' and *Leptospermum brachyandrum* 'Silver'.

Bottom: The landscape was designed to be low-maintenance and this was achieved by using plants such as *Eucalyptus leucoxylon* 'Euky Dwarf', *Dianella* 'Little Jess' and *Leucophyta brownii*.

'As above so below'. The
stillness of a Yarra Valley sunrise.
This view from the deck is
spectacular.

Pimelea nivea

Opposite
Clockwise from top left:
*Leucophyta brownii; Melaleuca
thymifolia* 'Pink Lace'; *Baloskion
tetraphyllum; Westringia*
'Deep Purple'.

The Synergy Garden

The Synergy Garden

This garden is an example of what happens when an architect (Zen Architects), a landscape designer and a client collaborate. It's a garden that is designed to not only complement the new home, but also be a driving force in its architecture.

The owners had lived in the area for sixteen years and were very connected to their local community. As their two children grew, they decided to stay and redesign their house and garden rather than move somewhere else. It was a very old home, with a completely overgrown garden. The owners' goal was to use the best possible sustainable practices and to encourage their children to get outside and interact with the surroundings.

A landscape designer usually joins a project after or near the completion of a build. The problem with coming in afterwards is that the whole landscape has already been manipulated, and the soil has possibly been contaminated. The topsoil has usually been stripped and taken away and you probably have to buy it all back. This project reinforced to me how beneficial it is to have the landscape and the house design integrated from day one.

An undertaking like this is all about project planning. The landscape design inspires the architecture, and vice versa. If the team and I are involved early on we avoid retro-fitting infrastructure. We've got to be realistic about logistics of course, and some things can be quite difficult. On this particular site we had an amazing established liquidambar tree (*Liquidambar styraciflua*) that was sixty-plus years old. It was going to be the main feature of the landscape, so we had to ensure it was protected during construction by putting in a tree protection zone.

The front garden is so different from the other front gardens on the street. Low, informal native plantings contrast with the mainly exotic scheme of the surrounding gardens. The owners didn't want to be closed off from their community. They hated the idea of blocking people out and living behind fences. Without a formal front fence, the landscape now merges with the streetscape and the owner says that people often stop for a chat in front of the house and admire the garden.

The owners were inspired to build a house that had a smaller footprint on the land than the previous one—it's important to leave space on a property for cooling our urban environment with plants. They've now also taken things to an exciting new level, where they're able to monitor how much energy is used and returned to the grid, and how much water is used and conserved within the property.

One of my favourite features is the vertical garden. It's actually running off a billabong. And it's not using power from the mains, it's running off solar power. The vertical garden represents a lovely symbiotic relationship, where there's a billabong that's supporting life while also creating an amazing green space that's cooling the building and creating beauty and biodiversity—there is a whole different habitat and microclimate just within that space. Conventional vertical gardens can be sustained in a variety of ways, such as being run off a hydroponic nutrient dosing system or irrigated pots. The billabong feeds

Previous pages
Light and shadows play in this
backyard oasis.

Opposite
The beautiful stone path leads
visitors through the front garden.
The warmth of the timber walls
is in harmony with the nature of
the garden.

water and nutrients to the vertical garden and then the water drains back into the billabong. You don't see this in any other vertical gardens around the world.

My team and I have had the opportunity to work with French botanist Patrick Blanc (who is regarded as the grandfather of vertical gardens) on multiple projects, such as the Melbourne Central Shot Tower vertical garden and the Trio apartments in Camperdown, Sydney. From these experiences we've discovered and developed new ways to implement more sustainable vertical gardens. The vertical garden we created here is 4 metres high and 2.5 metres wide.

We've selected plants for the vertical garden that were once indigenous to this area, such as *Brachyscome* and *Chrysocephalum*, the Australian native violet and *Doodia*, a type of fern. Different plants have different water requirements, so the plants at the top, which is drier, don't need as much water, while the plants at the base are more water-loving, because obviously there's more water flow at the bottom. Getting a vertical garden to look established will depend on the size of the plants used. This particular one took twelve months to settle in, but it is still quite young.

This whole landscape is being run off water that's collected from the roof. And after the vertical garden is irrigated, the water drains back down into the billabong and creates a flourishing habitat. It's doing two things at once. Anyone could have this working for them in their home. As long as you've got the catchment and you manage your water use, this system will even get you through times of drought.

I've had clients adapt their household water use in summer as a result of noticing that the water in their billabong has gone down, and realising it hasn't rained for a while. It's this sort of thing that helps make people aware of their water use in an urban environment. When they understand and observe it happen, they're not just being told it, they're living it.

The owners didn't want a classic chlorinated blue pool, they wanted a swimming environment that was unique for the family: a natural, chemical-free swimming pool. My company has seen an evolution with our billabongs, with people wanting to use them as a swimming environment. That changes the applicable regulations, because we then have to fence it and apply cutting-edge technology for cleaning the water. This has led us to undertake further research and development in Europe, where the natural pool industry has existed for more than thirty years. Within Europe there are in excess of 300 public natural pools, which is quite amazing. At the time of writing there is not one in Australia.

We build our pools in harmony with nature, which means in tune with the multitude of processes and phenomena that comprise natural, healthy water. As a result you don't need to use any chemicals when enjoying your pool, and no chemicals are discharged into our environment. Unlike conventional pools, we use a biotechnology that does not try to eliminate all life forms from the water in order to control potentially harmful organisms. Instead, it creates and maintains an environment that is in balance.

The key to this balance lies in the creation and maintenance of a low-nutrient environment, as can be found in clean rivers and in glacial and mountain lakes.

— — — —

'The billabong feeds water and nutrients to the vertical garden and then the water drains back into the billabong.'

— — — —

Opposite
We used indigenous plants to create this vertical garden. Species include *Agapetes meiniana, Chrysocephalum apiculatum* 'Silver Sunburst', *Scaevola aemula* 'Purple Fanfare', *Crowea exalata, Brachyscome multifida, Doodia australis, Rhododendron lochiae, Goodenia ovata* prostrate form and *Lomandra* sp.

Above: Even a small backyard can offer a balance of lifestyle and nature.

Right: The local ducks enjoy the water too.

Opposite
Banksia integrifolia, Derwentia perfoliata, Melaleuca thymifolia, Pycnosorus globosus and *Brachyscome multifida* have been planted along the fence to soften both the fence and the rocks.

The water quality in this garden's pool is exceptional. It's moving, sparkling, oxygen-rich water, which is clear and healthy.

The house is close to the beach, so for practical purposes we included an outdoor shower. The family can also us it to wash off before swimming in the natural pool. The shower is connected to a large reclaimed ironbark post, and we've used pebbles at the base. If you can access your hot water line from your house, you can easily create a hot shower in your backyard.

The smaller pond is the filtration zone. This is where all the filters are installed and this is what assists in cleaning the pool. Yet it's been made as a beautiful design feature next to the living room. Children love walking overthe stepping stones—it's like stepping over a creek.

This landscape provides something for everyone to observe, enjoy and engage with. You'll see various species of butterflies, for example; and in the afternoon, the sun comes in from an angle that sends an intricate pattern of rippling water onto the ceiling of the house.

The property has a north-facing winter courtyard that is amazing from a thermal point of view. The courtyard is constructed from brick, and the result is that it can be five degrees warmer in this space in winter. But, equally, the idea was that this landscape would provide lots of shade for summer. We therefore have the large, curving deck as the location for summer lunches under the ornamental grapevine.

I find the symbiotic relationship of the landscape to the house, and the way the landscape assists in cooling the residence, inspiring. Not to mention the vistas and the energy that have been created within the space. Being in the house is like being in the garden: the garden really serves as an extension of the internal living areas.

I think what we see in this house and landscape can be applied anywhere around the world. The property is even making money from energy; the owners are getting a credit from the power company. That's smart!

This pool evokes memories
of swimming in waterholes
as a child.

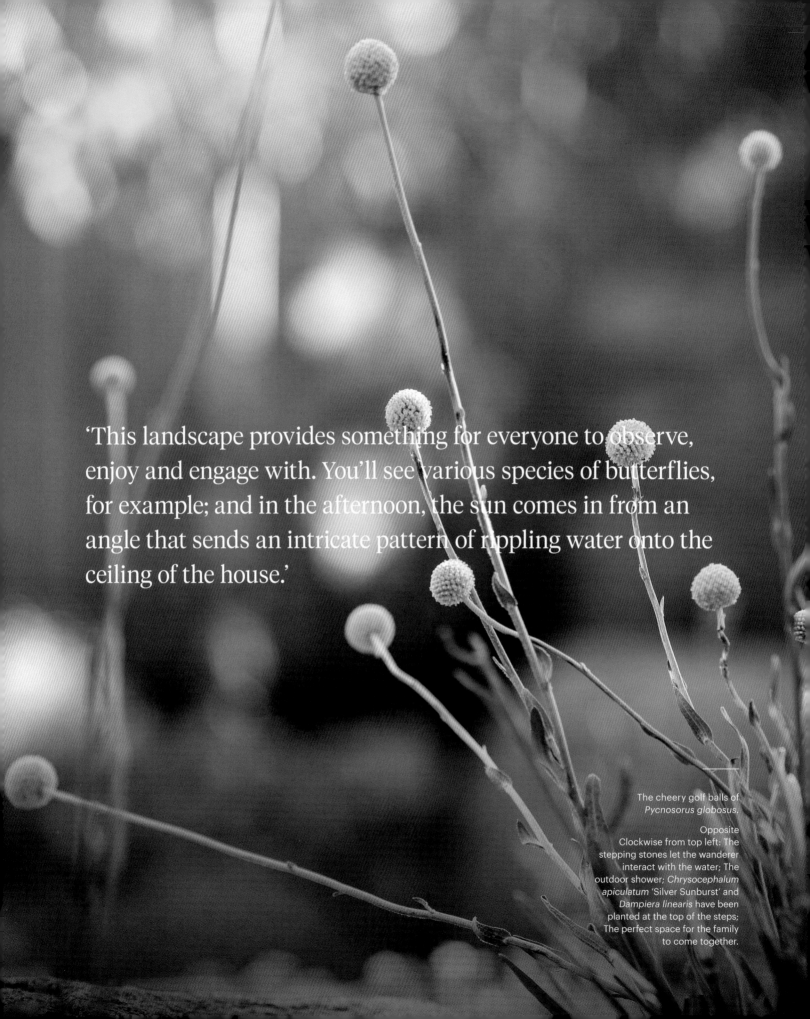

'This landscape provides something for everyone to observe, enjoy and engage with. You'll see various species of butterflies, for example; and in the afternoon, the sun comes in from an angle that sends an intricate pattern of rippling water onto the ceiling of the house.'

The cheery golf balls of
Pycnosorus globosus.

Opposite
Clockwise from top left: The
stepping stones let the wanderer
interact with the water; The
outdoor shower; *Chrysocephalum
apiculatum* 'Silver Sunburst' and
Dampiera linearis have been
planted at the top of the steps;
The perfect space for the family
to come together.

Dichondra repens loves to creep in between the rocks and contrasts beautifully with the colours in the granite.

Opposite
Top: This unique pool fence is a sculptural feature in itself.

Bottom: The silver leaves of *Chrysocephalum apiculatum* 'Silver Sunburst' provide a strong contrast to the green of *Mentha australis*. These low-growing shrubs soften the rocky hardness of the stream.

'The owners were inspired to build a house that had a smaller footprint on the land than the previous one—it's important to leave space on a property for cooling our urban environment with plants.'

— — — — —

Left: *Melaleuca thymifolia, Brachyscome multifida* and *Dianella* 'Little Jess'. These pretty plants soften the metal fencing and provide lovely bursts of colour in the garden.

Below: Reclaimed wharf timbers create a rustic fence.

Bottom: *Xerochrysum bracteatum* cultivar.

The Wetlands

The Wetlands

The opportunity to work with a historical landscape doesn't come around too often. Bolinda Vale is a large estate with a beautiful homestead built in the early 1800s using bluestone from the property. It has a traditional garden of exotics complementary to the house, an expansive lawn area, and a circular driveway lined with huge elms and oaks. The property sits on 5000 acres (2023 hectares).

After hearing one of my lectures, the owner went home and looked at her property with a new perspective. She realised she thought of herself as the custodian of Bolinda Vale. And that's what made her contact me and say, 'I've got a paddock we could do all this in!' She also mentioned she had 'a few rocks lying around the backyard'.

When I first saw the property, I couldn't believe the amount of rock we had available to work with in our design. 'A few rocks' was a huge understatement! And it was such beautiful rock. It had been stockpiled many years ago—the owners always viewed it as a hindrance; they couldn't see the true beauty and potential in these piles of stone.

Before we created our landscape, the area was a flat paddock. Now, it's come to life; we've opened up and expanded what was there.

This was a massive project. The planning and build encompassed a fifteen-month process—the build took a total of five months. Initially, I spent a lot of time looking at the forms and contours of the existing landscape, as well as drawing inspiration from the surrounding environment. This is one of the most critical design principles. You really need to spend time with certain properties to get a true understanding of the space, to be able to conceptualise what would work in relation to the scale of the site.

We wanted to design a landscape that connected perfectly with the environment. The placement of stone was based on existing outcrops, for example. We've also created a lot of contouring and mounding to direct water and to provide protection from prevailing winds.

It was imperative that the small details be executed at the same high standard, so that when you 'zoom in' from a couple of hectares down to a square metre, the quality is still there. That was a real challenge here, because of the scale of the build.

I wanted to design the landscape so that you have a glimpse of the main waterfall when you first enter through the gates to the residence. The idea was that you see a flow of water that entices you down into the landscape, into the experience.

There were quite a few other existing elements on the property that we were able to work around. It's amazing to imagine that there was once a tennis court surrounded by a cypress hedge where our spring is now located. I took inspiration for the spring from the remarkable bluestone rainwater tank that was built on top of a ridge to provide water pressure to the homestead in the 1870s. We replicated this beautiful circular form. The spring is surrounded by

— — — —

'When I first saw the property, I couldn't believe the amount of rock we had available to work with in our design. "A few rocks" was a huge understatement!'

— — — —

Previous pages
The billabong and curved boardwalk now occupy an area that was once just a flat paddock.

Opposite
A view from the billabong up to the historic homestead. The owner added a row boat.

Above: Rock stepping stones take you on a journey through the wetland. Species planted include *Lythrum salicaria*, *Triglochin procerum*, *Marsilea drummondii* and *Schoenoplectus pungens*.

Right: *Xerochrysum bracteatum* 'Sundaze' white.

Opposite
This dry creekbed channels water from the driveway into the wetland.

a circular avenue of oaks. This will create, in time, such a beautiful amphitheatre of vegetation.

People might be forgiven for thinking that I only work with Australian native plants. I do love them, but I also have a horticultural appreciation for the remarkable palette of plants and trees that are available. As you would expect with a historic site such as this, there are multiple avenues of exotic trees throughout the property, ranging in age from newly planted to a hundred years old. We have mirrored this element with our design for another area on the southern side of the works.

The existing English garden now flows into the new garden. The transition area from the formal garden close to the house to the native garden was linked via a dry creekbed, which was planted either side with a mix of exotics and natives. The owner's existing garden contained several plants that we could select for this transition, such as *Echium candicans* (pride of Madeira), and *Euphorbia*, *Cistus*, *Iris*, *Salvia* and *Sedum* species. We complemented these with plantings of purple-flowered *Patersonia occidentalis* as well as *Dianella* sp., *Doryanthes excelsa* (Gymea lilies) and kangaroo paws—to name only a few. *Lomandra* sp. and other grasses were planted to soften the rocks that were used throughout the design.

We planted lashings of Billy buttons (*Craspedia* sp.) and *Lythrum salicaria* to achieve the effect of a mass of soft yellow and purple colour. Further along the creek and garden beds we incorporated key feature plants for striking impact, such as grass trees (*Xanthorrhoea* sp.), huge bottle trees (*Brachychiton* sp.) and Gymea lilies.

The curved boardwalk is an interesting feature. At 20 metres long, it was inspired by the shape that the human form makes when lying down.

Detailed planning is critical for these projects, and they often require engineering solutions. The dam was built from our computer-aided design (CAD) plans, which were uploaded to the excavator—this then enabled the machinery to create the specified levels and gradients we needed.

A serpentine creekbed twists through the whole space. Water flows down off the roof of the homestead and off the driveway into the creekbed, and then down into the billabongs. These multiple water catchments also assist in providing water for the residents in the event of a bushfire. Unfortunately, fire is part of the reality of the property and its surrounds. This water will assist in reducing the intensity of a fire if one ever comes, because it has to travel in a northerly direction and pass over the wetlands.

Ease of maintenance was also one of our considerations for the team and me when we designed the garden. The lawns are mown with a ride-on mower, so the sweeping lawn area had to have an easy gradient. It was imperative that we factor in ongoing maintenance, because this is a rural working property, and available time and resources are at a minimum.

This is a very young garden—at three months old it's literally just at stage one of its life—but it works well with the existing heritage of the property. And it blends in with the surrounding English garden.

The owner's aim is to inspire future generations. She is building on the work begun by her husband's family, who have lived on the property since the 1800s. And her hope is that the next generation continues to build on what she's achieved. She also wants people to see what is possible. The family would like the property to be truly self-sufficient in the future, and are investigating how to take it off the grid and become more environmentally friendly. Currently, all the waterfalls, streams and night lighting are running off solar power.

Years ago this landscape was cleared, rock was removed, the site was levelled, and a monoculture of plants was created. The way this environment has now been transformed adds life to this once barren paddock.

Lythrum salicaria provides a seasonal burst of colour. The snaking boardwalk draws you into the landscape beyond.

'The opportunity to work with a historical landscape doesn't come around too often. Bolinda Vale is a large estate with a beautiful homestead built in the early 1800s using bluestone from the property. It has a traditional garden of exotics complementary to the house, an expansive lawn area and a circular driveway lined with huge elms and oaks.'

— — — — —

Left: This formal pond lets you hear the gentle sound of water before you enter the larger landscape, with its grand waterfalls. We planted *Cyperus lucidus* in the pond and *Baloskion tetraphyllum* surrounding it.

Below: This lawn area with its formal pond and plantings of *Quercus* (oaks) provides a formal transition from the grand bluestone homestead to the wetland landscape.

Bottom: The circular avenue of oaks surrounding the spring.

Every vantage point provides
a different view and feel.

Opposite
Clockwise from top left: The first
billabong; The rocks are placed to
direct water in curves and moves
just like a natural creek; Native
plantings among the rocks next
to the boardwalk; Plants such
as *Marsilea drummondii* grow
vigorously between the stepping
stones.

'The way this environment has now been transformed adds life to this once barren paddock.'

Top: A branch across the creek adds dimension and texture.

Bottom: *Persicaria decipiens* and *Eleocharis sphacelata* have been planted in this creekbed.

Opposite
The clear water lets you see every ripple on the creekbed.

Top: A summer afternoon, with the trees reflected on the surface of the billabong.

Bottom: Late afternoon, when the lights come on in the garden.

Opposite
Top: The large waterfall.

Bottom: This chunky boardwalk draws you into the expanse of lawn.

The Show Gardens

The Show Gardens

Melbourne International Flower and Garden Show

2009—Habitat

I had always wanted to exhibit at the Melbourne International Flower and Garden Show (MIFGS) at Carlton Gardens. For the 2009 show, we met with the event organisers and presented our concept. I had never exhibited a show garden, and I wanted to blow people away with our design.

A conventional show garden size is about 64 to 100 square metres. What we were proposing was close to 650 square metres. We'd told the organisers we wanted to do something bigger and better. I never knew there was a Best in Show there. I would have just been delighted with a gold! We were in the heart of the drought, and I wanted to create a design that inspired people to think about water-sensitive urban design and water efficiency, sustainability, urban greening—and connecting people back to nature. And they were excited by the concept, because it was different. It was the first exhibit that had chickens in it!

I wanted the best possible site, at the start of Main Avenue, so when you came out of the main doors of the Exhibition Building and looked across through the fountain you'd see our installation.

I originally wanted to encourage people to walk through the whole landscape, but that wasn't allowed because of occupational health and safety concerns. So I selected a site on a corner that was viewable from three sides, and I designed a viewing platform so that people could still experience it and be engaged.

I don't really like trends. Nature doesn't have trends. I had seen a really beautiful Japanese design in the past, but nothing like the complexity of what we were about to do. What we were pushing wasn't the trend. It wasn't a minimal landscape, it wasn't a monoculture—we had seventy different species. I wasn't sure whether even at MIFGS people would engage with it and like it.

It was a really complicated site to build on, because there's a significant level change. I wanted to incorporate something people would recognise as iconically Australian—a billabong—and the level change allowed us to create a beautiful upper pool, which had a hot outdoor shower immersed within it. The water then made its way down to a meandering stream into a lower billabong. These days I hear people from all over the world say, 'I want an Australian billabong!'

We set some strict criteria in terms of selection of resources and materials. We wanted 95 per cent of all the resources and plants to come from within a 100 kilometre radius of the site. That made us very critical in our material selection: aggregates, rocks, mulches, plants, how we built retaining walls, rock work, reclaimed timbers, all the different components had to be sourced locally.

I wanted to recreate a self-sustaining household, and we did that by including a chook pen, an orchard mound and a vegetable garden that undulated along one side of the creek. We even had a clothesline as a reminder: you still need to have a functional and practical landscape. I often hear people at show gardens say, 'I love these designs but they're just not practical—where does your

Previous pages
A lush sanctuary, MIFGS 2011.

Opposite
The curved sunset platform—the epicentre of our 2009 design. It was inspired by sunset at Uluru. Glass chandelier by Miles Johnson.

clothesline go?' The clothesline emerged through a beautiful piece of stone, and that rock has been reused in the Produce Garden.

We had to disguise the backdrops of the other competitors, so to do that we built a massive 5 metre wall of solar power panels. This generated enough power to run the entire site, removing the need for mains power. All the pumps, the lighting and the hot water service were run by solar-generated power that was stored on-site in a bank of batteries.

I actually did ask whether we could tap into the downpipe of the World Heritage-listed Exhibition Building. This was not possible, unfortunately! I still wanted to show how the system could function and sustain itself, how it would replenish, and in theory this would be from the residence. But instead, we had a large rainwater tank. Aquatic plants in the billabong provided a filtration zone to absorb nutrients from the run-off water, which assisted in cleaning the water. It also created a habitat for frogs, insects and microorganisms. The aquatic plants were selected for their ability to tolerate periods of both inundation and dryness, so they would be resilient, lying dormant in times of drought when the water had completely evaporated from the billabong.

When full, the upper billabong overflowed into a creek that aerated the water as it channelled through a secondary filtration zone and meandered to the lower billabong. The lower billabong provided a larger catchment zone that was governed by the same principles as the upper billabong, with the added bonus of providing a natural pool for swimming. The capacity of the lower billabong enabled a significant amount of water to be captured for irrigation, and also for fire protection, if required.

We wanted to incorporate components from other projects we'd worked on over the years, such as the stepping stones in the lower billabong. A granite waterfall provided an aesthetic and acoustic feature, and it was operated using power generated by the adjacent solar wall.

The whole landscape was permeable. The majority of the time our landscapes are 80 per cent permeable, if not 100 per cent.

For this build we brought in eleven truckloads of rock—that's 120 tonnes. We actually had the privilege of doing a mock build at Hanson Quarry in Lysterfield. We carried out all the placement of the rock, and identified and numbered each one, so that when it came time to building it at the Carlton Gardens we could execute it efficiently. We had to coordinate the delivery of types of rock based on the logistics of the build. It's the same principle we later took to Chelsea, but there we had 400 tonnes of rock.

The epicentre of this design was our sunset platform, which was inspired by a dinner my wife, Sarah, and I had watching the sunset at Uluru.

This landscape was carefully designed to work with the existing site, taking into account the World Heritage-listed Plane Tree Avenue and the beautiful natural slope of the site (a 1.7 metre fall over 44 metres).

When I was in the initial discussions with the event organisers I told them of my vision of suspending a glass chandelier from a tree. They said we wouldn't be able to touch the tree. They never allowed anything to be attached to the

Opposite
Top: A view of the granite waterfall, powered by the solar panels behind it.

Bottom: The green wall, irrigated from the billabong, breaks up the wall of solar panels. These panels generated enough power to run the whole site.

trees. Whenever we design anything, our philosophy is to consult arborists first. So we had arborist Roger Greenwood work with us. He produced a 100-page report detailing where this chandelier could go. The proposal was to attach it to a network of tree branches, which would evenly disperse and spread the weight. Each evening we'd lower it to take the weight off the trees.

Having produced this report, we met with Melbourne City Council, asking for permission to attach the chandelier to the tree, using appropriate slings and applying best practice arboricultural techniques. Roger also surveyed the root systems of the surrounding trees using a ground-penetrating radar and produced a three-dimensional map. Any of our large boulders would be positioned away from tree root systems, and all the rock on our site would be placed on compaction mats, which dispersed and spread the load of the rock so it didn't impact on any one point. Because of that planning and the care we took, we were given permission.

My brother Miles worked on this glass sculpture, and it took him more than two months to create it. The chandelier had in excess of 130 pieces of handblown glass inspired by the kangaroo paw flower, red and gold. It was situated directly in the centre of the installation, below the sunset platform—and as we had anticipated, every night the chandelier had to be lowered. The hanging point was right above the centre of the sunset platform. The whole landscape design had to evolve from that specific point.

The sunset platform was made of recycled timbers. It allowed for a perfect sitting area right in the centre of the landscape, with the chandelier above, and water, rock and foliage surrounding.

For the planting design, I played around with idea of a meadow and used kangaroo paw, *Ptilotus* sp. and *Brachyscome* sp. I wanted to show the life cycle that occurs within nature, so we didn't just feature the hero plants, we also brought in their small offspring, demonstrating how nature evolves and grows. For example, we incorporated some advanced bottle trees (*Brachychiton rupestris*), and had adult specimens right down to little juvenile ones. We designed our wildflower planting placement in groups, and actually dispersed them so they appeared to be spreading out within the landscape, as happens in nature. Over the years we had taken photos in order to observe how this occurs in places such as the Kimberley and other desert environments, and we used those as points of inspiration in our planting design and placement.

MIFGS regulations meant that all the plants had to remain in their pots, so we had to disguise the containers. If one pot was seen through the mulch or the aggregate, you actually lost points. This could be the difference between winning a gold or a silver, so attention to detail was crucial.

We also had a bush beehive and our pathways were permeable—a rocky cobble with an aggregate between. And for the first time we saw how beautifully ferns worked around water for this installation. I had the idea then to use them at Chelsea. We had two vertical gardens at the rear of our installation, which were being sustained from the water and nutrients from the billabongs.

The team and I were awarded gold and Best in Show. My next goal was Chelsea. We had to wait five years, but that allowed me the time to put the planning in place. And to research, research, research!

— — — —

'We wanted to incorporate components from other projects we'd worked on over the years, such as the stepping stones in the lower billabong.'

— — — —

Opposite
Clockwise from top left: The rugged stone path is permeable and the water message is reinforced by the visible water tank; Closer detail of the granite waterfall, powered by the solar panels; The firepit surrounded by lush ferns; Stepping stones through the billabong.

2011—Bathe

We went from showing a 650 square metre installation at MIFGS in 2009, down to a 64 square metre installation in 2011. Our aim was to compress it and show how you could actually have a show garden with the same vision and principles, but on a smaller scale.

Over the years I've had people question me about using rock, because it's not sustainable. So in 2011 I decided to build a garden out of waste material—out of old red bricks that had been thrown out, as well as rubble and concrete. David Long had designed and created a wave wall, out of rubble, influenced by the devastating Japanese tsunami that year.

We only used one piece of stone from a quarry, which before we obtained it was going to be crushed into road base. An enormous amount of energy would have gone into that, so we salvaged it. It's such a remarkable piece of stone, and it's now a fishing platform in a private lake in Somerville, Victoria.

We created some floating steps out of cut blocks of concrete that had been removed from construction sites. Our mulched aggregate was concrete rubble. We created waterfalls and used just the bare minimum of pebbles.

The reason I wanted to do this was to challenge myself as a designer with material selection, to see how it would all work and how the public would respond. (In fact, originally we were thinking of building Chelsea out of waste material, too.)

We couldn't excavate at MIFGS, so we had to work within the limitations. We created a plunge pool that was chemical-free, using simple technology including a natural filtration zone system. Clusters of native rushes and sedges, such as water ribbons, were positioned in the filtration zone bordering the natural pool. Concrete pavers that had once lined suburban footpaths became almost unrecognisable in their new location, aggregated into a waterfall over the pool and assisting in aerating the water.

Zen Architects, with their focus on contemporary sustainable architecture, designed the 'home', which was a shade structure. And it was really our first opportunity to work on a show garden with an architectural firm.

Added to the rooftop was a moss wall and a vegetable garden, and both were sustained by water from the natural pool. This symbiotic integration provided nutrients for the plants in the green wall, and added a further natural filtration zone for the pool.

The varied environments and weather conditions that make up the Australian landscape were represented in the planting design, ranging from lush ferns to bright kangaroo paws and striking grass trees.

I had been doing a trial growing moss in the form of a vertical garden, and so at the back of the structure we installed a moss wall. One of Australia's most renowned and talented horticulturalists, the late Colin Campbell, said it was one of the most amazing horticultural feats he had seen.

Opposite
Recycled materials such as bricks, rubble and concrete were a key feature in the Bathe garden. The plunge pool is chemical-free and uses a natural filtration system.

Something that I've found difficult to achieve in a lot of our show garden exhibits is educating the public about our design principles—about how sustainability should be an underlying factor in every design. I always present talks, and my team and I make ourselves available to the public to ensure our message is clear. Sustainability should be the number one criterion of design. We received the sustainability award for this show garden.

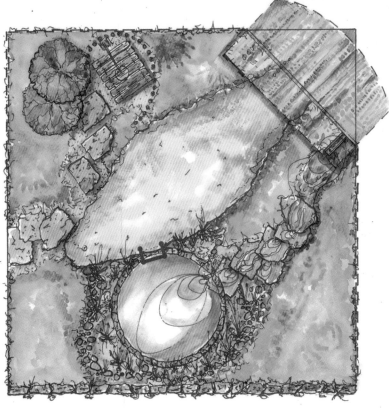

Above: Sculptor and stonemason David Long created the 'Wave' wall. The recycled brick wall frames the plunge pool. Recycled concrete was used to build the cascading waterfall.

Top left: Watercolour layout of the Bathe garden.

Left: The outdoor shower.

Melbourne International Flower and Garden Show

2012—Equilibrium

After we won the sustainability award in 2011, the savewater! Alliance—a not-for-profit association that promotes water efficiency—approached us to say *they* had really wanted that award! They asked if we'd like to collaborate with them in 2012. There were a lot of Melbourne water retailers at MIFGS who were showing the public what they could do in their area. My vision was to bring together all the water retailers in Melbourne (including Melbourne Water, and the Victorian Government), to work collaboratively and to show one vision. That's how we came up with Equilibrium.

Equilibrium contrasts two gardens of equal size, one a conventional Australian backyard covered in concrete, using exotic plants, and with water sources leading to drains. The other is a sustainable landscape that creates water and habitat corridors in an integrated way using different local water sources—bringing communities back into equilibrium.

The 'before' garden was basically an 8 metre by 8 metre space attached to a pre-fab house designed by Prebuilt, who sponsored us. This incorporated a normal backyard, which had a large concrete driveway, a clothesline, small garden beds and a bit of lawn. All the PVC pipes of the downpiping were purposely placed above the ground, as if you had x-ray vision and were looking into your stormwater pipe network.

Next door we had exactly the same house, but this one collected roof water and illustrated the whole integrated water cycle management message. When the tank overflowed, the water ran down a stream to a billabong that began to rise; when that overflowed, the water was directed under the road through a rain garden and into an existing lake in Carlton Gardens. It demonstrated the story of water—how we need to clean water, slow it down, and actually treat it before it exits into our waterways.

We also had a lot of trees. Deciduous species or Australian natives help cool our cities down. It's all about urban greening.

Colin Campbell saw we had a hydrangea growing on the edge of our billabong, and he asked why we would include it in our otherwise native garden. I explained that because the colour of the flower changes depending on the pH of the water, it's an indicator of water quality. We can monitor the pH level of our water, see whether it's acid or alkaline, based on the colour of the hydrangea.

We were presented with the sustainability award and Gold Medal Show Garden. The then Premier of Victoria, Ted Baillieu, presented me with the award. When I gave my acceptance speech, I took my most recent water bill out of my pocket and said to him, 'I'm really upset about how expensive my water bill is, I got it last night … It's a total of $13.50 for the quarter'. I wanted to show how having an integrated water cycle management system like that can reduce your water footprint.

Equilibrium inspired us to remember how important it is to educate the public about conserving water and how to apply that in your own home.

Opposite

Top: Equilibrium shows that an urban backyard doesn't have to be sterile to be functional. On the right is a sculpture by David Long.

Bottom: The boardwalk takes you through the garden and past the stream. On the left-hand side of the boardwalk, a hydrangea has been planted to indicate water pH.

Top: The rear of the residence, where you can enjoy the tranquility of falling water as soon as you walk out of the back door. Advanced *Banksia integrifolia* have been planted. The sand beach flows into the billabong. The beach adds a sense of calmness and it's also tactile. To the right of the rainwater tank are raised herb tubs by Joost Bakker.

Bottom: The stone steps were made from locally sourced mudstone slate and were designed to look as natural as possible. The rocks were carefully selected and the steps were handcrafted by David Long. They allow access to the show garden. The steps are purposely angled to slow you down as you enter the garden.

Opposite
Top: The gorgeous trunk patterns of *Eucalyptus pauciflora*. You can see the overflow pipe from the rainwater tank where, once the tank is full, water is channelled through the stream and flows down to the billabong.

Bottom: This simple waterfall was made from a flat sheet of mudstone slate to create a beautiful curtain of water. The aim was to create something that was achievable in a suburban backyard. We've used aquatic plants such as *Triglochin procerum* and *Baloskion tetraphyllum* in the billabong.

The Chelsea Flower Show 2013

The Chelsea Flower Show 2013

*The Trailfinders Australian Garden presented by Fleming's
Designed by Phillip Johnson*

Getting to Chelsea had always been my dream. My journey would not have happened without Wes Fleming, the owner of Fleming's Nurseries in Monbulk, Victoria—and my neighbour. Fleming's Nurseries had been taking the Australian gardens to Chelsea since 2004.

The reason Wes goes to Chelsea is to promote the Australian horticulture industry. It allows us to develop relationships with governments, and it allows us to be involved in policy-making—which is important, because that's where big decisions about sustainability and the future of our environment are made. Wes and I work so well together because we have similar philosophies. I think his determination to construct a garden on the other side of the world is incredible. He says that going to Chelsea is like an addiction—it's like being part of a big family. Over the years he has nurtured and taken some of the top landscape designers in Australia: Ian Barker, Mark Browning, Jamie Durie, Jim Fogarty, Dean Herald, Jason Hodges, Jack Merlo, Scott Wynd. Wes describes Chelsea as the Olympics, the Ashes and the Oscars for horticulture.

The English had been regarded by many as the best in the world when it came to horticulture and landscape design. No Australian had ever won Best in Show at Chelsea before 2013, even though Australians had won multiple golds and silver gilts. Up until 2013, Wes was convinced it would never happen.

My journey to Chelsea started the day Wes and I bumped into each other at one of our local coffee shops. He said, 'Phil, I think it's time we do it. It's the last time we're going to go to Chelsea and I want you to do our last ever show garden'. I wanted to execute Best in Show for Wes and the Fleming's team. If I got him believing in my vision, I knew we were going to pull this off. We were going to work hard every minute of the day, and strive for utter perfection.

I had the privilege of going to Chelsea twice before exhibiting, in order to research what worked there, to check out our competition, and to listen to people's reactions to what they saw. I was told, 'You'll never beat the English at their own game'. To embark on something you're told you can't actually win ... it strengthened my drive to do it.

We were about to undertake the most ambitious and complicated build in the history of the Chelsea Flower Show. It was bold, challenging and risky. I was aware that sustainable design was becoming increasingly important, but I wasn't sure if the English would like what we were planning to do.

The building timeline was critical. The team and I had to start planning two years in advance, and then the intensity of the planning increased in the lead-up to Chelsea. We broke every detail of the build down into specific sections. Meticulous planning will help you win. The other thing we had on our side was the fact that we are a design and construction company. We don't just design, we design and build, so I knew that everything I'd come up with could be implemented. But I was pushing my personal benchmark to excessive levels.

Previous pages
Who would believe this landscape is in the middle of London and the Thames is just behind it? This garden was all about reconnecting people with nature.

Opposite
The Waratah Studio overlooks the serene billabong. *Dicksonia antarctica* appears very much at home growing between the rocks.

'I love this design, and how it slices through the natural pool creating different sections. It curves and takes you past my favourite aspect, which is looking back across at the BBC through the billabong.'

The lovely curved boardwalk takes the explorer on a journey through the garden. I love how the 9 tonne boulder connects with the sand and water. On the left is where the filtration zone is hidden, below the aquatic plantings.

Opposite
The view from the BBC studio lets you see the whole garden.

The curved sunset platform provides a place to take in the view of the waterfall and Waratah Studio. The entire build took just seventeen days.

Our design was incredibly ambitious. The build itself was going to be three times the size of my top billabong in Olinda, and the whole project was going to be bigger than my home garden, which took me a year to build. And the Chelsea garden had to be built in seventeen days!

So it was all about the plan. Our builder, David Pontifex, from Atkinson Pontifex, had been to Chelsea on four occasions. We also had Michael Khalil, the site manager from our company, who was running the project; and Vaughn Greenhill, my general manager who was involved in the project management and planning side of things; as well as Leanne Gillies, from Fleming's Nurseries; and David Long, the stonemason. The six of us shut ourselves in a room and began planning. We broke the build into stages, down to the smallest possible detail you could ever imagine. That was the first of many very late nights!

Eighteen months before the show, Wes and I met with the Royal Horticultural Society, where I had the opportunity to present my vision. They fell in love with our concept (which had evolved a few times), and with my passion and drive to inspire more sustainable design and connect people back to nature. They told me this was exactly the direction they wanted to take the Chelsea Flower Show.

The Australian garden had only moved to two different sites over eight years of involvement, but the Royal Horticultural Society encouraged the change in site to assist with the logistics of the build. This enabled us to work on the rock embankment.

It was the site of the very first Chelsea Flower Show gardens 100 years ago, which were rock gardens built into the contour of the embankment. Our design was for a 12 metre by 24 metre build, with a level change in excess of 13 metres from the bottom to the top of the Waratah Studio. My design just got bigger!

We wanted to exhibit a functioning system, to show how it could operate and come alive and be self-sustaining when it rains. So I was adamant that we should also harness water off the surrounding rooftops of the BBC, or the Royal Horticultural Society offices. We were able to do it, but it certainly complicated things.

However, Chelsea nearly didn't happen for us. We spent a lot of time trying to work out how we could get funding. Over the years, Fleming's have underwritten it many times and put in excess of $2 million into Chelsea. This year, due to the financial hardship caused by the GFC, they decided they were not going to do that—so we had to find additional funds.

We had a deadline, and if we hadn't had confirmation by then that the Victorian Government would assist in sponsorship, the project wasn't going to commence. Wes and I had a meeting with the then Premier of Victoria, the Honourable Ted Baillieu, and presented him with our vision and concept.

Just before I went into this meeting, I saw a kookaburra—they have always been my lucky charm. I gave the Premier a lemon myrtle plant as a gift, for him to grow. I told him I wanted to showcase how good Australia is at sustainable design and put Victoria on the map.

If the money didn't come through, Wes and I would have had to cover the costs to send the equipment back to Australia, because the containers had already

The Chelsea Flower Show 2013 Landscape Plan

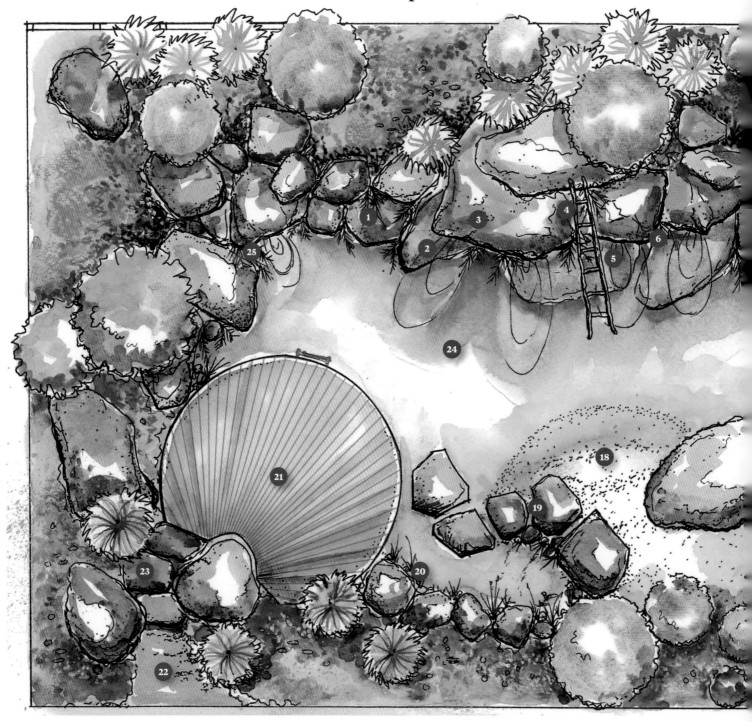

LEGEND

1 Plants emerging from crevices in face of gorge
2 2.5 metre high sheet waterfall
3 Diving rock
4 Timber ladder for climbing in and out of Billabong
5 3.8 metre high waterfall
6 3.6 metre high waterfall
7 Water tank
8 Stepping stones
9 Studio above this area
10 Stairs to access Studio
11 Ornamental screens
12 Stone wall
13 Hot outdoor shower
14 Stone steps to access vegetable gardens
15 Filtration zone
16 Boardwalk constructed from reclaimed timber
17 Stone steps to access boardwalk
18 Sandy beach gently sloping into the Billabong
19 Stepping stones
20 Aquatic planting zone
21 Sunset Platform with timber pool ladder attached
22 Access from residence
23 Stone steps to access Sunset Platform
24 Billabong (natural swimming pool)
25 Stream

Viola hederacea creeps into the nooks and crannies between the rocks and pebbles.

Opposite
Every pebble is visible in the billabong. A 7 metre ladder provides access to the the top of the waterfall. The tree ferns have been grown at angles to replicate how they would grow in nature.

been sent to the UK. It was a very stressful time. However, I had kookaburras coming into my garden and appearing on branches, left, right and centre during this period, which made me say to myself, 'Hang in there! It's going to happen!'

We had told the Victorian Government that this was the last year Fleming's Nurseries was going to Chelsea, as well as the 100-year anniversary of Chelsea. And the government came back and said yes—they would support us in some way to make it happen.

The government funding helped, but it was only a small amount and we had to find more. I travelled around the country trying to get financial sponsorship and support for the project. I had clients assist us who believed in our vision, and friends and family too. The Victorian Minister for Water, the Honourable Peter Walsh, was also a great support. We had suppliers provide products at no cost, and we had architects and builders donate their time.

The crew didn't get paid to be over there, it was a voluntary crew. We were all over there to win. We had more than a hundred people help us make this project happen over the two years. And the eighteen volunteers who came with us were exceptional.

In choosing who would come, we selected people who were multi-skilled, from plumbers who were also excavator operators, to carpenters who were also able to multi-task. We had in excess of 50,000 plants that had to go in, so we had to pull in all our resources.

The BBC organised a crew to film us in Australia before we left. This helped introduce us to the English audience. The segment communicated the sustainability message, what we were trying to achieve, and our approach. The crew visited Fleming's nurseries for the first time and they also came out to my home garden.

It's not really the done thing to say, 'We're going to Chelsea to win Best in Show'. But we were saying it! We had put in two years of dedication and planning. We had to stay positive.

All our equipment had to leave three months before the show in huge containers on ships, so in the lead-up from December we'd been doing all the pre-fabrication at Atkinson Pontifex's offices and workshop in Cheltenham, Victoria. I had been told to pre-fabricate as much as possible, so that we could basically just drop it in when we arrived and fix it all together.

There was an enormous amount of preparation: packing equipment, writing shopping lists, making sure we had every single thing ready. We had to record everything; we could not forget one tool. Everything was documented. Everything had to be coordinated, and that's where Fleming's Nurseries' experience showed, because they'd been to Chelsea eight times before. They knew the process inside out.

The first time we brought the whole team together in Atkinson Pontifex's offices, we held a presentation to inspire the team members. The last time I had been to Chelsea I'd looked at the craftsmanship, the detail of the plants, the finishing, the garden edging, the plant material used and the planting themes, and I observed the public's reaction: what they loved and what they didn't.

Clockwise from above: A watercolour perspective of the Chelsea garden; *Rhodanthe chlorocephala* and *Leptospermum scoparium* 'Red Damask' scramble among the trunks of the juvenile *Brachychiton rupestris*; Flowerbuds of *Xerochrysum bracteata* 'Sundaze' and mass planting of *Pratia pedunculata* around the base of juvenile *Brachychiton rupestris*; Brendan Stemp's ladder from the Sunset Platform allowing ease of access to the natural pool; My favourite area—the shade grotto. We created a microclimate that would be a cool space to be in on a hot day. Large boulders retaining the edge of the gorge surrounded the grotto, and we built a curved sandstone wall. Growing out of the nooks and crannies we had violets and ferns—both shade-loving plants.

I described these obsessive observations to the team, in addition to my design vision, in order to prepare them for what we were up against.

Everyone was aware of how ambitious this build was. For example, we needed to disguise all the BBC buildings behind us at Chelsea, and that's why we were going to construct such a tall rock gorge. I also wanted to create a dramatic backdrop. And that backdrop allowed us to plant in all the nooks and crevices within the rock gorge, just as occurs in nature.

But the *pièce de résistance* was the Waratah Studio, created from reclaimed, offcut aluminium. I'd worked with architect Dylan Brady from Studio 505 on his own home project, and we'd seen how exciting architecture and landscape design could be when they intersected. So we developed the idea of the studio.

The waratah was the first flower my father gave my mother when she returned home after living in London for eighteen months, in the days before they were married. They wrote love letters to each other every week she was away. My father met her at the airport with a bunch of waratahs, and they got engaged. And that's where the idea for the Waratah Studio originated. Dylan and his team looked at the geometry of the flower and created an abstract twist on it.

I suggested to Dylan that we design the studio so it would draw the Queen to our garden. I was hoping we could get her right up into the actual studio. With this in mind, I researched her eye height: it's approximately 5 feet 3 inches. (I later had a conversation with the president of the Royal Horticultural Society and she told me that the Queen thought it was amusing that I had discovered her eye height through a Google search!) The Waratah Studio was designed so that when Her Majesty stood in the centre of the studio and looked out, all the timber petals would disappear from her line of sight and she would have the most beautiful uninterrupted view of the entire landscape. Dylan also designed a louvre system, which allowed evaporative cooling throughout the Waratah Studio, via the microclimate that was generated by the billabong.

As Dylan described it, although the studio appeared incredibly solid and dense from the outside, when you were inside the structure it felt completely transparent, and connected you with the landscape. The studio design was driven by geometry. The shape was a sphere that was split into two slices, a four-side slice and a three-side slice, and from within that we excavated a cube and a sphere. Together their intersections revealed the structure and padding of the studio pod. The pattern that was cut into the petals was also geometrically driven. The geometry was once again reinforced as you walked around the studio and viewed the patterns; the centre of the sphere was also made apparent.

I even asked my dad to do a cloud study on canvas that we could have sitting on an easel within the studio. That's the level of detail I went to.

A corner of the Waratah Studio was supported by three boulders. They were selected to look like they were balancing on top of one another. I've seen this sort of obscure and unbelievable rock formation occur in nature. We also had a functioning hot outdoor shower, which was heated on-site using solar power.

Brendan Stemp, one of the best timber sculptors in Australia, made the ladder. We needed a 7 metre high ladder. That's the measurement from the bottom of

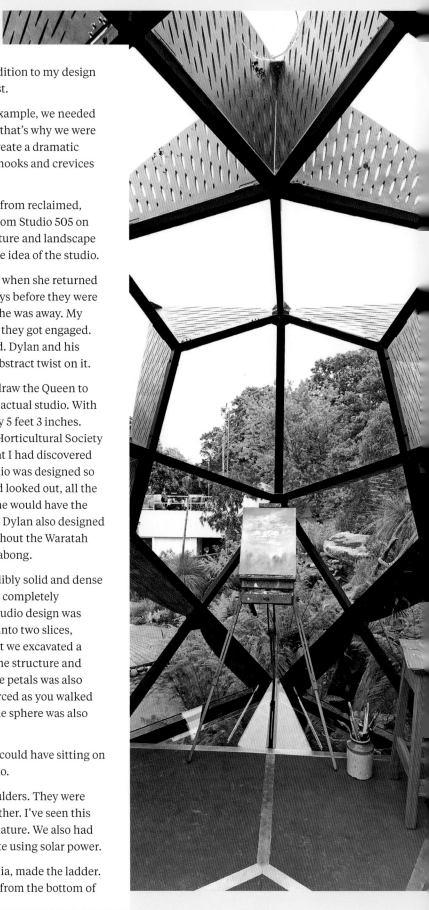

Above: The 'petals' of the Waratah Studio are angled so that when inside, you have an uninterrupted view of the garden but are shielded from view from the outside.

Left: The vibrant green of *Cyathea australis* and *Dicksonia antarctica* contrast beautifully with the steel staircase by Lump.

Opposite
The Waratah Studio is the architectual work of Studio 505. This shows the view from the studio overlooking the garden. My father, Colin Johnson, painted a 'cloud study' as a work in progress.

the billabong to the top of the gorge. We required it for access, to show the judges how you can actually maintain the landscape at the top of the gorge.

The garden featured our signature stepping stones, which meandered across to the sand beach, inspired by a squeaky beach at Wilsons Promontory in Victoria. The stones led up to the beautiful Sunset Platform, which was based on the one we presented at the Melbourne International Flower and Garden Show in 2009. This design sliced through the natural pool, creating different sections. As it curved it took visitors past my favourite aspect, looking back across at the BBC through the billabong.

We knew that what was going to help us win Chelsea were the plants. The English are so remarkable at creating their meadows, wildflowers and herbaceous borders. They have such a wonderful array of plants and flowers. And what we wanted to do was translate that and create a wildflower meadow with an Australian twist, using our unique species. All I had to do was find out where we could get these plants from.

I worked very closely with Leanne Gillies from Fleming's, who had been involved in all of their previous Chelsea Flower Shows. A simple way to develop your palette is to cut out pictures of the plants and arrange them on a page to see how they will look. There was a lot of attention to detail—from how a little fern frond unwinds and grows, to how a native violet exists under a certain edge of a billabong.

The planting palette for Chelsea was probably the most complicated thing to get right. We came up with our dream selection, which combined the best, in my opinion, of all Australian plants. But I could only find five different species out of 150 in the UK and Europe. So I had to work backwards to devise our palette. We had to source plants that were in propagation, growing within the UK and Europe. This was where the knowledge and networks that Fleming's had developed over the previous eight years were paramount.

The lead-up to Chelsea that growing season was the worst possible spring and winter the UK had experienced in fifty years, with adverse light and temperature conditions. I knew I could build the gorge, and I knew our carpenters and architects could make the forms and structures. But the question was: were we going to be able to execute horticultural perfection?

Some of Australia's best regarded native planting experts, such as Angus Stewart and Rodger Elliot, helped us try to source things in the UK and Europe. As part of our plant reconnaissance trips, Wes, Leanne and I went to Italy and Spain multiple times, and travelled throughout the UK.

We located a massive bottle tree in Sicily. I wanted something that was large and bulbous. But then we also wanted some juvenile specimens. We found some amazing multi-trunked grass trees (*Xanthorrhoea glauca*), which were in flower. They were the tallest flowering plants at Chelsea. I couldn't believe it. So all these little things aligned along the way.

I was excited by the eucalypts we found growing in Hillier Nurseries in the UK, including *Eucalyptus pauciflora* subsp. *debeuzevillei*—my favourite. It's a type of multi-trunked snow gum that grows in the high country of Australia, and it also thrives in the UK because of the cold climate. The gum we chose

was 9 metres tall, and it was pivotal in softening the edge of the Waratah Studio—the multi-trunked formation also created a lovely sculptural effect.

Eighteen months beforehand, I had met Dave Root (what a great name for a horticulturalist!) from Kelways nursery. He's the number one grower of tree ferns in the UK. I showed him pictures of my own home in Olinda, and how the tree ferns emerge from crevices, how they grow outwards on an angle and align themselves parallel to the ground. I wanted to soften the rocky gorge at Chelsea with tree ferns too. But we needed to get that angle right. I also told him I wanted to keep the dead fronds on the sides of the ferns. I was trying to mimic a natural system, and what I'd seen before was this type of fern pruned to perfection. And that doesn't occur within a natural system.

This whole time, we were working under an immense level of pressure. If one load of rocks didn't arrive, or if it rained at the wrong time, we would not be able to build. We were also anxious about the containers coming from Australia, which held almost everything we needed: from hammers and drills, to timber, cement in moisture-proof bags, the Waratah Studio, duct tape and rags. If the containers hadn't arrived, we wouldn't have had anything to use!

The rock gorge that was the framework of our installation was created from rock sourced from throughout the UK. The column and pillar rocks that formed our waterfalls were salvaged from a landslip that had occurred fifteen years earlier, and they'd been transported to the depot of the suppliers, CED, in Castlecary in Scotland. The rocks had just been sitting there for all that time, growing moss, waiting for us to build an Australian gorge with Scottish rock!

We did the mock build at Castlecary in November 2012. My team and I moved 400 tonnes of rock in 13 days. We had to devise a safe and secure lifting technique for our column and pillar rocks. We also had everything surveyed, every single rock, large or small, so we knew the shape, orientation, connection points with surrounding rock, the weights and the lifting points. Then all the rocks were broken down into the various loads that would be required at certain times: fourteen different loads that would be delivered into the heart of London. We then had to wait six months until we built it all again at Chelsea.

Just before we left Australia for the UK, Wes Fleming received a letter from the representatives of Her Majesty the Queen informing us that we were on her schedule for Chelsea. She would be coming by to view the Australian garden, since it was the last time Fleming's Nurseries would be sponsoring it, after nine years' attendance. They requested additional information, so we sent seventeen pages of detailed material.

On the plane heading to London, we wore the uniforms that Fleming's always organised. The team had to leave in three different groups. David Long, our stonemason, departed a month early to source the materials and work on the stone wall with our English stonemason counterparts.

The first thing we did when we arrived in London was review all our nurseries, so that we could scrutinise the quality of our plant stock. Our stonemasons had arrived in Scotland by then to load all the rocks onto the trucks to start the journey down to London. I was begining to get very nervous, especially when I saw how under-developed the flowers were. We were expecting a lot more

Opposite
Ptilotus exaltatus created quite a buzz among the fascinated Chelsea crowd. Also shown here are *Brachyscome* 'Mauve Mystique' and *Podosperma gnaphaloides* (syn. *Podotheca gnaphaloides*).

growth—these were the bedding and wildflower plants that were pivotal to our design. We didn't need them for another three weeks, but I worried that they wouldn't be ready.

We reviewed the aquatic plants at Anglo Aquatic Plant Co and discovered they hadn't had enough warmth to really develop the flower that was required. Everything just hadn't had enough sunlight to help dense growth and flower. However, we did have an advantage over our competitors, because a lot of our other plants were coming from elsewhere in Europe where the climate was a lot warmer, such as Spain.

By this time, everyone on the team had arrived. David Pontifex was managing the studio build, staircases, posts, boardwalks and Sunset Platform. David Long managed the stonemasonry work. Steve Weber was involved in all the rock placement—the slinging of boulders and craning into position—his role is referred to as a dogger (or rigger). Leanne Gillies was in charge of the plants. Michael Khalil coordinated all activities and managed the implementation of the works. And the rest of the team, who'd never worked together, were about to embark on the most ambitious, complicated build in Chelsea's history. Every single person had to understand the exceptional standard of quality that was required.

Then the time came to start building. We had to work on really bad soil. The day we were meant to start we found out from Thames Water that we weren't allowed to build on our original proposed site, due to the fact we had the London sewer directly under what was going to be our gorge. The last thing we wanted was for the gorge to collapse into the London sewer!

We had to move 50 metres away. That threw every measurement, and all the detailed documentation that our design studio had worked on, out the window. It put extra stress on us to adapt our designs from a site that was originally flat, to a site that now had significant level change.

This land had been excavated and backfilled probably close to a hundred times. So, when excavation started, we had to come up with a lot of engineering solutions and control measures to stabilise it, and make sure it was safe when we were craning in the large pillars and columns.

First, we lined the site with multiple layers of geotextiles. We needed that structural integrity beneath it, and we had to make sure there were no foreign objects underneath the billabong that could possibly penetrate and pierce the liner, because the last thing you ever want is a leak. That's the word you never mention: leak.

When the crane arrived, it was almost as high as the London Eye. It was only supposed to be there for four days, but it stayed for twice as long because we underestimated the complexity and logistics involved in getting everything on top of the gorge. We used the crane to move additional material all around the site.

The first rock arrived. It weighed 6 tonnes, and this was the most critical piece of stone. The rock had to be placed in a position that was no more than 5 millimetres out, and it had to be the perfect level. It took us close to five hours to place that first rock. It was imperative we got it right, because it was the one everything else was built around. We still had hundreds of rocks to come in.

Our ferns also had to arrive early; I was a bit nervous about this, because they hadn't had the chance to harden and completely open out. They really don't like being exposed to the extreme winds that can occur on a construction site at the Royal Hospital Chelsea grounds. We had to make sure we stored the ferns in the same orientation as they'd been positioned inside the greenhouse, so that there was no change in the growing directions of the fern fronds. A fern frond can change its growing direction very quickly, because it grows towards the light. That can be the difference between gold and silver gilt. So we had to position all these tree ferns at obscure angles, to replicate the same alignment that would have occurred in the nursery.

The waterfalls took a while to get right. We had four of them. The main waterfall had specific requirements: we needed the right overhang of rock so that when the water spilled, it hit the rock below that we'd selected. If it hit that rock at the wrong point, it could have dispersed water out too far, or it could have made the decking wet and caused too much noise.

We were also showcasing the first underwater garden at Chelsea, using aquatic plants, which are very important in helping to clean the water and create another habitat in the ecosystem.

During this time, David Pontifex was working on the Waratah Studio. Concrete had been poured to support all the infrastructure behind the scenes.

Just so you can get your head around the complexity of even getting a plant off a truck—it took us about three hours to do this with our hero bottle tree without damaging it. It had arrived wrapped, and looked like it had been pruned like a bonsai, but Leanne swore that as soon as we undid all the packing the shape would come back, and she was right.

My favourite area was the shade grotto. The English love their grottoes, so we thought we would build one with an Australian twist and create a microclimate that would be a cool space to be in on a hot day, with fern fronds, and a staircase inspired by my spiral staircase at Olinda. Large boulders retaining the edge of the gorge surrounded the grotto, and then we had a curved sandstone wall. Growing out of the nooks and crannies we had violets and ferns—both shade-loving plants.

Previous Chelsea Flower Show designers had told me that it's really important to spend an hour each day sitting and enjoying your creation. One of my favourite spots to sit was the sandstone wall, where I could look out through the grotto and into the billabong. Once the build was complete, I made sure I did that every day.

Wes arrived towards the end of the build, and his energy really lifted us. He is just the master of planting. Both Wes and Leanne are both highly skilled at planting, and they made our palette blend together beautifully.

We planted warmer colours in the foreground and cooler colours in the background. But that had to evolve as we went on, because we were running out of stock. We were concerned that we wouldn't have enough quality flowering plants in the foreground to really wow the public, so we had to use our hero plants sparsely and stop them from being used everywhere else, as was our original plan. The 'wow' plant for the English was *Ptilotus exaltatus*. We also

used *Rhodanthe chlorocephala* and a range of kangaroo paws. My job at this point was to watch the planters and how the patchwork of plants was blending together, and to make sure you couldn't distinguish between who put in the plants: you can usually see the difference between the planters, it's like handwriting.

I was also very concerned that the plants weren't going to really settle in. I had never planted a massive wildflower meadow like this. There were 20,000 plants that I'd never had the opportunity to use before.

The way the English work, you need to have the plants in four daysbefore the judging, so they have time to settle. We were running out of time, and this wasn't going to happen. Wes assured me that as soon as the plants were in the soil and were irrigated, they would settle in.

The planting of the aquatic plants within the billabong was especially difficult. We had people who spent the whole day planting this delicate plant palette in the half-filled billabong, in extremely cold temperatures. One of the hardest things was to make the plants look instantly natural, especially around the billabong, the filter zones and the stepping stones.

At Chelsea the public isn't encouraged to connect with a garden in an up-close way, but I really wanted them to. I was keen for them to actually reach out and touch the bottle tree. We also positioned a boulder right on the edge of the installation so they could feel and connect with it too.

Three days away from completion of the build, we were all utterly exhausted, but the media attention we were receiving throughout the UK was massive. People were starting to talk about what we'd created. There was a buzz around our garden.

That day I was inside the Waratah Studio when I saw the show manager trying to grab my attention. I noticed security guards and additional people around. And then out of the blue, Prince Harry arrived. Wes and I spent about half an hour with him, walking around our site and taking him on a tour. He said that if we'd had a rope swing he would have jumped into the billabong! Prince Harry asked so many questions about what we'd designed. I asked if he'd be interested in seeing inside the Waratah Studio, and explained that it had been built with the Queen, his grandmother, in mind. We asked if he could take off his work boots before he walked in, and he did, and stood in the Waratah Studio in his royal purple socks! Later I was told that Prince Harry spoke to Her Majesty about the studio, and she said, 'But Harry, you saw the vision from my eye height, but you're not my eye height. How did you manage it?' And he replied, 'Oh, Grandma, I just squatted down to five foot three!'

Prince Harry came down and introduced himself to every team member, and took a team photo. We were actually competing against him—his foundation sponsored one of the other gardens—but he was very generous with his time, and he motivated all of us. The team was, from this point on, re-energised. You could see it on everyone's face, it was exactly what we needed. That visit from Prince Harry was, I believe, the turning point in our build. We were so utterly worn out, and his arrival at that time gave us the morale boost we needed.

What I really wanted to showcase was the quality and importance of craftsmanship within the build. We didn't use manufactured stone imported

Opposite
A side view of the waterfall
framed by *Dicksonia antarctica*.

Mass planting to create
a beautiful meadow.

Opposite
Clockwise from top left:
Xerochrysum bracteatum
'Sundaze' magenta;
Leptospermum scoparium
'Red Damask'; *Xerochrysum
bracteatum* 'Sundaze' white;
Anigozanthos flavidus 'Big
Red'; *Ptilotus exaltatus*; *Cotula
coronopifolia* and *Rhodanthe
chlorocephala*; *Rhodanthe
chlorocephala* subsp. *rosea*;
Podosperma gnaphaloides
(syn. *Podotheca gnaphaloides*).
Centre: *Brachyscome* 'Mauve
Mystique'.

from other countries, we used local stone that was worked and shaped to create these extraordinary masterpieces. The English are the masters of stonework. We had three exceptional stonemasons. David Long ran the team, with Alistair Tune and Callum Gray. Callum actually came from Scotland, and he brought local knowledge that helped us in working with this stone. Their remarkable skill was showcased in our step work, in our placement of rock throughout the landscape and gorge, but most of all in the exquisite dry stonewalling of the grotto.

At this point we were filling up the billabong. It was holding water, which was a massive relief. Then it came time to turn on all the waterfalls. Everything had been building up to that point. The flow of water over the face of the gorge was perfect—it was exactly what I wanted. But then we noticed a serious problem. The water level was dropping significantly. It was the most dreaded scenario you could possibly imagine: we had a leak! Or so we thought.

To put this into perspective: it was the night before judging, and over the last few weeks we had moved in excess of 400 tonnes of rock over this butyl rubber membrane. The crane had already left before the leak was discovered. We thought it had to be somewhere behind the gorge. At one point we had water running down next to the entrance of the BBC. That didn't look good.

Every single stage of this build had been photographed for historical reference, so I knew if something went wrong I could call on a photo, which would hopefully assist in locating the problem. That night I went through the photo archives of the build to try to identify what might have happened. I saw that there were times when we were climbing on PVC plumbing lines for the waterfalls, using them as a ladder. Could this be the problem? I gave the photos to the team to use.

We had to keep calm and go through the process of identifying the problem. Finally we discovered that it was a combination of where the liner was fixed to the entrance of the waterfall, and how plants were planted around it—they were pushing down on the liner. This is the problem in building a show garden—we couldn't fix the liner like we'd normally fix it, because we had to dismantle it in five days' time. Over the next day, the team adjusted the liner, secured it better, and monitored the system. When you commit to building the most ambitious show garden in 100 years of Chelsea, on the other side of the world, and on such a steep site, you've signed up for some challenges.

We didn't realise until just before we completed the build that the public couldn't see the water in the billabong because of the gradient change from the original site. So the Royal Horticultural Society provided an elevated viewing platform, and this allowed two vantage points.

And then finally it was complete. I still can't believe we did it! I had achieved my ultimate dream. There were times when I wasn't sure if we would be able to pull it off, and I'd never been so exhausted in my entire life.

The judging is based on five criteria: brief/purpose, overall impression, overall design, construction and planting. Before the head judges do their adjudication, the assessors come and report to the head judges on who should win. The designer usually only has two minutes with the assessors to explain

what has changed in the design. This is important, because we are judged according to the brief; if we change anything, we have to communicate that to them quickly and succinctly. In my meeting with the Royal Horticultural Society in February I was told they don't allow animals at Chelsea. But I asked them if I could make an audio recording of frogs from my garden in Olinda, and have that playing in surround sound throughout the garden. I wanted to demonstrate the by-product of creating these amazing environments, that frogs come back to habitats like this. They were excited. So, late one night before we left Australia, I made an audio recording on my boardwalk at home in Olinda. The sound of the frogs started just before the assessors arrived, which was bizarre and surreal—because I was on the other side of the world, and my frogs were there! When they came in I purposely took my shoes off so that I could walk through the environment barefoot, connecting with the earth. I told them about the things that had evolved and altered.

One of the main things I stressed to the assessors was that it is possible to create this type of landscape in an urban environment. I live with a landscape like this. I had to make sure they knew it was achievable.

The media day is the number one gala function to go to, and it launches the social calendar. We had visits from celebrities such as Ringo Starr, Jamie Oliver, Natalie Imbruglia and Helen Mirren. Princess Beatrice came over and introduced herself to everyone.

Taking my parents through the garden for the first time was really humbling. My mum nearly couldn't make it across—two days before departure she was told she couldn't fly due to illness, but in the end she managed to get clearance, and I was overjoyed to have them there.

Late in the afternoon on the media day, the whole place was locked down for the Queen's visit. The day before, Wes had pulled me aside and said, 'You need to work out who you want to meet the Queen'. Wow, this was a big decision! I asked, 'Couldn't we have more than one person?' But unfortunately not. I asked Wes who he was introducing, and he told me it would be his wife.

I really wanted to have the site manager who ran the project. I wanted Leanne, who had been going to Chelsea for nine years. I also wanted David Pontifex, who had been to Chelsea four times. And I wanted David Long, the stonemason, as well as other representatives from my company. But in the end I selected my wife, because if it wasn't for her support, I wouldn't have had the ability to make this project happen.

The Queen shook our hands. She asked me to explain what I'd designed. 'Your Majesty, I've designed this landscape to connect humanity back to the beauty of nature. To show how important it is to add biodiversity and greening to our urban environment.' She then asked, 'What's the sound of those frogs I hear?' I replied, 'Your Majesty, one night I was doing an audio recording of the sound of the frogs at my garden next to my billabong in Australia. What you hear is the by-product of what we create, these beautiful frogs. I wanted to have this audio recording throughout the landscape so you can hear that. So it's a little touch of my home'. We could see she enjoyed hearing about our creation.

Opposite
Cotula coronopifolia and
Brachyscome multifida.

We had been told a couple of days before, 'Whatever you do, don't encourage the Queen to go into the garden'. But Wes came forward and asked, 'Your Majesty, would you be interested in having a closer look?' The Queen jumped at the opportunity. She went straight up the steps. A representative of the Royal Horticultural Society hurried after her and said, 'Your Majesty, you're not supposed to enter the garden', and she replied: 'I want to see this garden, I can't see it from here'.

I walked beside her up the steps, just in case. And then I had a few minutes with her on the boardwalk, having a wonderful discussion ranging from how we harnessed water from the rooftop of the BBC and designed the billabong to fluctuate, to our plants, our natural pool and the Waratah Studio. That time spent with the Queen was such an honour.

The next day was awards day. The whole team was dressed in their uniforms. Nicki Chapman, who was hosting the BBC live broadcast of the Chelsea Flower Show, handed us an envelope and said, 'Mr Johnson, here's your award'. I opened it and we looked at it—it was gold!

We were over the moon! Champagne corks popped and we all began hugging and congratulating each other. I started being interviewed. I was looking around, and there was still a lot of other media there, but I thought they were just interviewing us for the gold. Then, while I was being interviewed, I was interrupted. It was Nicki. I had goose bumps. She said loudly, 'Excuse me, Mr Johnson, I forgot to give you something'. And then she handed me the Best in Show award.

How can I describe this moment? We were jumping up and down, it was as if we'd won an Oscar. I was utterly elated. There were hugging, tears and euphoria. I love how Wes Fleming described it: 'We are the Usain Bolts of horticulture and landscape design'.

I later found out that the BBC had scripted the announcement of the award deliberately, to make us wait. The drama of TV! That five-minute wait probably did long-term heart damage though.

Over the years, Wes Fleming has often been asked how he would react if he won Best in Show at Chelsea. Well, he just ran around in laps. I was so unbelievably happy for him. Wes Fleming deserved this.

And then Tim Wilkinson dived into the billabong, wearing just his jocks and the Chelsea hat. Four times. This image went viral. On the last dive, the reporters asked him what his name was—and he told them it was Phillip Johnson. Luckily he followed it with, 'Only joking'. But later I had to jump in as well, to christen the billabong. The whole team did.

It felt like Wes and I did about 300 interviews that day. The judges' feedback was that the energy and soul created in this landscape were truly inspirational. It had soul and beauty. Maybe that was why the Queen wanted to come into our garden. It was the first time in the 100-year history of Chelsea that all the judges had agreed unanimously on awarding Best in Show. And they had made that decision as soon as they all got back to the adjudication room.

Opposite
Clockwise from top left: The solar panels assist in running the pumps for the waterfalls and night lighting; The hot outdoor shower; The rock stepping stones take you through the billabong to the sandy beach; Detail of waterfall. The waterfall creates a mist that allows these ferns to flourish in the perfect microclimate.

One thing the judges did was a reference check on was how I used the tree ferns. Some were slightly submerged in water within the billabong. So the judges sent out emails around the world to tree fern experts to check that they are capable of growing in water. They should have just looked at my own home in Olinda! I've got about twenty growing at the edge of the water, slightly submerged in my billabong.

One of the hardest things was the demolition of the project. It was a terribly sad day when I had to say goodbye to this creation. I was told not to be there, because everyone knew how much it would shatter me. But I don't know how it could have been any easier for my colleagues. On the last day of the show it was beautifully sunny, after weeks of cold. All the plants were auctioned off. It gives me some sense of relief that now parts of our garden have been dispersed around the country.

Chelsea has been the pinnacle of my career. When I think back to it, I am just amazed by what you can do when you have an incredible group of people working together towards one vision and goal.

And as I said to Her Majesty the Queen, I wanted to do this to inspire people and connect them back to the beauty of nature.

It took me months and months to recharge after I arrived home. So more than ever before, I was overjoyed to be back in my healing garden at Olinda.

Looking down on the Sunset Platform.

An English Garden

Water Diagram

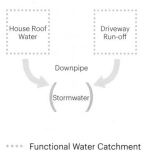

House Roof
Water

Driveway
Run-off

Downpipe

(Stormwater)

- •••• Functional Water Catchment
- ( ) Functional Waterway
- ➡ Water Direction

Water Table

Annual rainfall	867 mm
Roof catchment area	392 m²
Other hard surface area (e.g. paving or concrete)	90 m²
Potential water to be collected off roof per annum	339,864 litres
Driveway catchment area	66 m²
Potential water to be collected off driveway per annum	approximately 57,222 litres
Tank capacity	—
Billabong capacity	3000 litres
Size of property	643 m²
Permeability % of area	15%

My Home

Plant List

Acacia cognata
Acacia melanoxylon
Cyathea australis
Dichondra repens
Dicksonia antarctica
Eucalyptus regnans
Lomandra confertifolia subsp. *rubiginosa*
Scleranthus biflorus
Telopea speciossima 'Shady Lady'
Wollemia nobilis

Water Table

Annual rainfall	**1165 mm**
Roof catchment area	**350 m²**
Other hard surface area (e.g. paving or concrete)	**10 m²**
Potential water to be collected off roof per annum	**407,750 litres**
Driveway catchment area	**400 m²**
Potential water to be collected off driveway per annum	**approximately 466,000 litres**
Tank capacity	**73,000 litres**
Billabong capacity	**230,000 litres**
Size of landscaped area and house*	**4200 m²**
Permeability % of area	**91%**

* Total property area is 7 acres (2.8 hectares)

Water Diagram

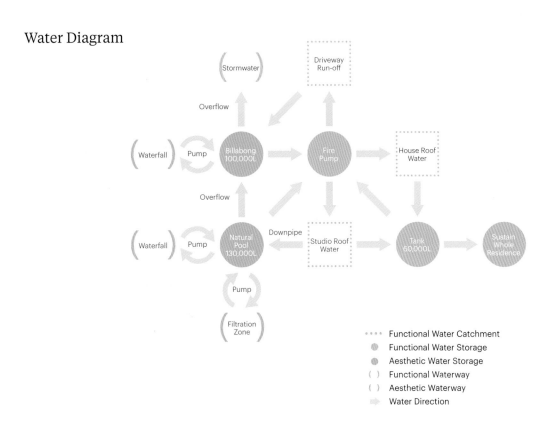

The Urban Kimberley Garden

Plant List

Acacia glaucoptera
Anigozanthos flavidus
Banksia integrifolia
Carpobrotus rossii
Correa alba
Dichondra repens
Leptospermum sp.
Myoporum parvifolium
Poa poiformis
Xanthorrhoea minor

Water Diagram

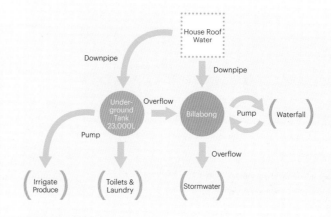

••••	Functional Water Catchment
◗	Functional Water Storage
◗	Aesthetic Water Storage
( )	Functional Waterway
( )	Aesthetic Waterway
➡	Water Direction

Water Table

Annual rainfall	**695 mm**
Roof catchment area	**183 m²**
Other hard surface area (e.g. paving or concrete)	**—**
Potential water to be collected off roof per annum	**127,185 litres**
Driveway catchment area	**35 m²**
Potential water to be collected off driveway per annum	**approximately 24,325 litres**
Tank capacity	**23,000 litres**
Billabong capacity	**10,000 litres**
Size of property	**851 m²**
Permeability % of area	**74%**

An Indigenous Garden

Plant List

Austrostipa scabra subsp. *falcata*

Chrysocephalum semipapposum

Doodia media

Eucalyptus camaldulensis

Poa ensiformis

Poa labillardieri

Pycnosorus globosus

Rubus parvifolius

Triglochin procerum

Triglochin striatum

Water Table

Annual rainfall	732 mm
Roof catchment area	400 m²
Other hard surface area (e.g. paving or concrete)	80 m²
Potential water to be collected off roof per annum	292,800 litres
Driveway catchment area	50 m²
Potential water to be collected off driveway per annum	approximately 36,600 litres
Tank capacity	13,000 litres
Billabong capacity	41,000 litres
Size of property	1000 m²
Permeability % of area	93%

Water Diagram

House Roof Water

Downpipe

Tank 13,000L

Pump → Toilets & Laundry

Overflow

Billabong 1 16,000L

Waterfall

Billabong 2 25,000L

Overflow → Stormwater

- ···· Functional Water Catchment
- ● Functional Water Storage
- ● Aesthetic Water Storage
- ( ) Functional Waterway
- ( ) Aesthetic Waterway
- ⇨ Water Direction

The Rock Garden

Plant List

Acacia pycnantha
Atriplex rhagodioides
Carpobrotus modestus
Craspedia paludicola
Eremophila decipiens
Poa labillardierei
Rhagodia spinescens
Themeda triandra
Wahlenbergia stricta
Xanthorrhoea minor

Water Table

Annual rainfall	595 mm
Roof catchment area	300 m²
Other hard surface area (e.g. paving or concrete)	40 m²
Potential water to be collected off roof per annum	178,500 litres
Driveway catchment area	1500 m²
Potential water to be collected off driveway per annum	approximately 892,500 litres
Tank capacity	335,000 litres
Billabong capacity	200,000 litres
Size of landscaped area*	5000 m²
Permeability % of area	93%

* Excluding the dam, total property area is 400 acres (162 hectares)

Water Diagram

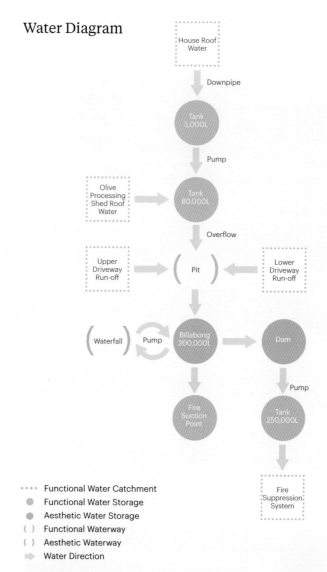

Functional Water Catchment
Functional Water Storage
Aesthetic Water Storage
( ) Functional Waterway
( ) Aesthetic Waterway
Water Direction

A Produce Garden

Plant List

Acacia glaucoptera
Allocasuarina grampiana
Baeckea linifolia
Baloskion tetraphyllum
Calothamnus quadrifidus grey leaf form
Chorizema cordatum
Eucalyptus pauciflora subsp. *debeuzevillei*
Grevillea 'Bonfire'
Hakea 'Burrendong Beauty'
Lomandra patens

Water Table

Annual rainfall	720 mm
Roof catchment area	173 m²
Other hard surface area (e.g. paving or concrete)	22 m²
Potential water to be collected off roof per annum	124,560 litres
Driveway catchment area	5 m²
Potential water to be collected off driveway per annum	approximately 3,600 litres
Tank capacity	17,600 litres
Billabong capacity	12,000 litres
Size of property	650 m²
Permeability % of area	69%

Water Diagram

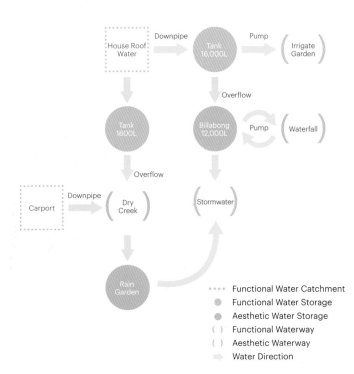

Functional Water Catchment
Functional Water Storage
Aesthetic Water Storage
( ) Functional Waterway
( ) Aesthetic Waterway
Water Direction

A Meditation Garden

Plant List

Ammobium alatum
Anigozanthos 'Big Red'
Banksia robur
Baeckea linifolia
Epacris longiflora
Eucalyptus preissiana
Guichenotia macrantha
Meeboldina scariosa
Myoporum floribundum
Thomasia sp.

Water Table

Annual rainfall	**867 mm**
Roof catchment area	**530 m²**
Other hard surface area (e.g. paving or concrete)	**6 m²**
Potential water to be collected off roof per annum	**459,510 litres**
Driveway catchment area	**120 m²**
Potential water to be collected off driveway per annum	**approximately 104,040 litres**
Tank capacity	**13,000 litres**
Billabong capacity	**70,000 litres**
Size of property	**4046 m²**
Permeability % of area	**84%**

Water Diagram

House Roof Water

Downpipe → Billabong 30,000L
Downpipe → Billabong 40,000L

(Waterfall) ← Pump ← Billabong 30,000L
Billabong 40,000L → Pump → (Waterfall)

Overflow

Driveway Run-off → Dry Creek ← Billabong

Studio Roof Water

Dry Creek → Stormwater

Dry Creek ← Tank 13,000L ← Downpipe ← Studio Roof Water

Tank 13,000L → Irrigate Garden

**** Functional Water Catchment
● Functional Water Storage
● Aesthetic Water Storage
( ) Functional Waterway
( ) Aesthetic Waterway
➡ Water Direction

The Fern Garden

Plant List

Adiantum raddianum
Asplenium australasicum
Blechnum moorei
Cheilanthes myriophylla
Dicksonia antarctica
Goniophlebium subauriculatum 'Knightiae'
Microsorum pustulatum
Platycerium superbum
Polypodium formosanum
Polystichum setiferum

Water Table

Annual rainfall	**867 mm**
Roof catchment area	**232 m²**
Other hard surface area (e.g. paving or concrete)	**—**
Potential water to be collected off roof per annum	**201,144 litres**
Driveway catchment area	**37 m²**
Potential water to be collected off driveway per annum	**approximately 32,079 litres**
Tank capacity	**12,000 litres**
Billabong capacity	**3000 litres**
Size of property	**720 m²**
Permeability % of area	**63%**

Water Diagram

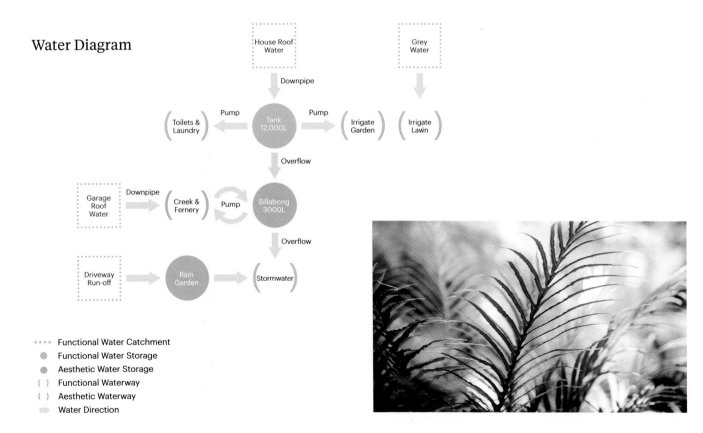

- •••• Functional Water Catchment
- Functional Water Storage
- Aesthetic Water Storage
- ( ) Functional Waterway
- ( ) Aesthetic Waterway
- ⇨ Water Direction

Lubra Bend

Plant List

Acacia aphylla

Acacia glaucoptera

Banksia blechnifolia

Banksia petiolaris

Banksia spinulosa 'Birthday Candles'

Eucalyptus lacrimans

Eucalyptus yarraensis

Leptospermum brachyandrum 'Silver'

Meeboldina scariosa

Themeda triandra

Water Table

Annual rainfall	**734 mm**
Roof catchment area	**900 m²**
Other hard surface area (e.g. paving or concrete)	**20 m²**
Potential water to be collected off roof per annum	**660,600 litres**
Driveway catchment area	**1500 m²**
Potential water to be collected off driveway per annum	**approximately 1,101,000 litres**
Tank capacity	**100,000 litres**
Pools and wetland capacity*	**1,450,000 litres**
Size of landscaped area only**	**8500 m²**
Permeability % of area	**89%**

* Calculated on new and old landscaped area

** Total property area is 300 acres (121 hectares)

Water Diagram

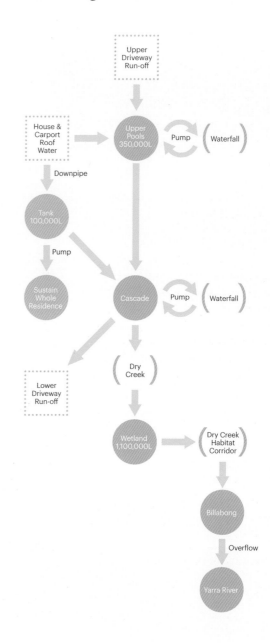

•••• Functional Water Catchment

⬤ Functional Water Storage

⬤ Aesthetic Water Storage

( ) Aesthetic Waterway

➡ Water Direction

The Memorial Garden

Plant List

Allocasuarina grampiana

Brachyscome multifida

Corymbia ficifolia 'Baby Scarlet'

Hymenosporum flavum

Leptospermum morrisonii 'Copper Crest'

Persoonia pinifolia

Scaevola aemula 'Mauve Clusters'

Scleranthus biflorus

Spyridium coactilifolium

Xerochrysum palustre

Water Diagram

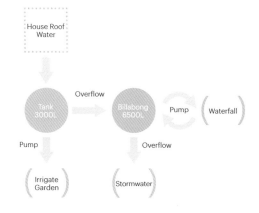

.... Functional Water Catchment

◐ Functional Water Storage

◑ Aesthetic Water Storage

( ) Functional Waterway

➡ Water Direction

Water Table

Annual rainfall	**587 mm**
Roof catchment area	**171 m²**
Other hard surface area (e.g. paving or concrete)	—
Potential water to be collected off roof per annum	**100,377 litres**
Driveway catchment area	—
Potential water to be collected off driveway per annum	—
Tank capacity	**3000 litres**
Billabong capacity	**6500 litres**
Size of property	**470 m²**
Permeability % of area	**64%**

The Birthday Garden

Water Diagram

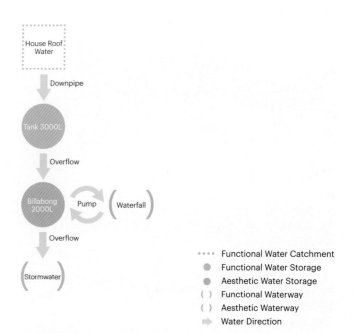

House Roof Water

↓ Downpipe

Tank 3000L

↓ Overflow

Billabong 2000L   ⟳ Pump ⟳   (Waterfall)

↓ Overflow

(Stormwater)

····	Functional Water Catchment
◉	Functional Water Storage
◉	Aesthetic Water Storage
( )	Functional Waterway
( )	Aesthetic Waterway
➡	Water Direction

Plant List

Acacia leprosa
Anigozanthos flavidus 'Big Red'
Chrysocephalum apiculatum
Eucalyptus leucoxylon 'Euky Dwarf'
Hardenbergia violacea
Lomandra confertifolia 'Wingarra'
Ozothamnus diosmifolius 'Radiance'
Pycnosorus globosus
Xerochrysum bracteatum 'Cockatoo'
Xerochrysum bracteatum 'Dargan Hill Monarch'

Water Table

Annual rainfall	**587 mm**
Roof catchment area	**200 m²**
Other hard surface area (e.g. paving or concrete)	**4 m²**
Potential water to be collected off roof per annum	**117,400 litres**
Driveway catchment area	**—**
Potential water to be collected off driveway per annum	**—**
Tank capacity	**3000 litres**
Billabong capacity	**2000 litres**
Size of property	**440 m²**
Permeability % of area	**54%**

The Evolving Garden

Plant List

Acacia aphylla

Acacia cognata

Anigozanthos flavidus 'Big Red'

Backhousia citriodora

Carprobrotus rossii

Dichondra repens

Eucalyptus leucoxylon subsp. *rosea* 'Scarlet'

Eucalyptus pauciflora 'Little Snowman'

Poa labillardieri

Stylidium graminifolium

Water Table

Annual rainfall	**649 mm**
Roof catchment area	**351 m²**
Other hard surface area (e.g. paving or concrete)	**77 m²**
Potential water to be collected off roof per annum	**227,799 litres**
Driveway catchment area	**56 m²**
Potential water to be collected off driveway per annum	**approximately 36,344 litres**
Tank capacity	**40,000 litres**
Billabong capacity	**55,000 litres**
Size of property	**1560 m²**
Permeability % of area	**69%**

Water Diagram

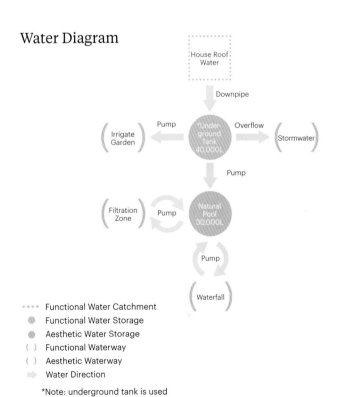

- **····** Functional Water Catchment
- **◉** Functional Water Storage
- **◉** Aesthetic Water Storage
- **( )** Functional Waterway
- **( )** Aesthetic Waterway
- **➡** Water Direction

*Note: underground tank is used for toilets and to irrigate garden

The Turtle Habitat

Plant List

Acacia baileyana prostrate form
Banksia ericifolia
Banksia repens
Banksia spinulosa 'Stumpy Gold'
Bulbine bulbosa
Chrysocephalum apiculatum 'Golden Buttons'
Dampiera stricta 'Glasshouse Glory'
Eucalyptus mannifera 'Little Spotty'
Leptospermum brachyandrum 'Silver'
Lomandra confertifolia 'Grey Cascade'

Water Diagram

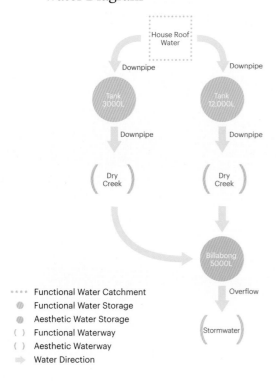

•••• Functional Water Catchment
◍ Functional Water Storage
◍ Aesthetic Water Storage
( ) Functional Waterway
( ) Aesthetic Waterway
➡ Water Direction

Water Table

Annual rainfall	**587 mm**
Roof catchment area	**211 m²**
Other hard surface area (e.g. paving or concrete)	**22 m²**
Potential water to be collected off roof per annum	**123,857 litres**
Driveway catchment area	**24 m²**
Potential water to be collected off driveway per annum	**approximately 14,088 litres**
Tank capacity	**15,000 litres**
Billabong capacity	**5000 litres**
Size of property	**590 m²**
Permeability % of area	**56%**

Turtle Facts

Graham and Jill have both eastern longnecks and Murray River turtles living in the backyard. Both species are endangered.

The eastern longneck is also known as the eastern snake-necked turtle. They are endemic throughout most of Victoria. Originally the Yarra Valley and Maribyrnong never had a turtle population, but they have spread and are now found throughout these areas. They can travel long distances across dry land looking for new waterholes or nesting areas. They grow to around 26 centimetres long, and eat invertebrates, tadpoles and small fish. They catch their quarry by striking like a snake.

Murray River turtles are common turtles that grow up to 34 centimetres long. They are omnivores, feeding mainly on water plants and algae, but they will also eat molluscs, yabbies and carrion. They can live to be more than 100 years old.

The Bushwalking Garden

Water Diagram

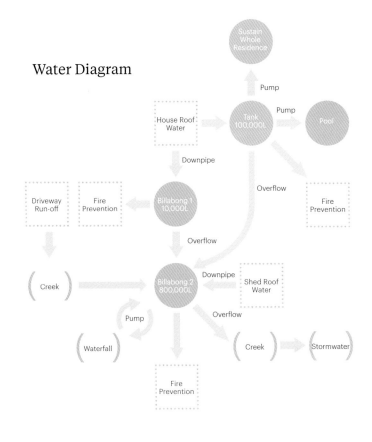

Sustain Whole Residence

Pump

House Roof Water → Tank 100,000L

Pump → Pool

Downpipe

Overflow

Driveway Run-off ← Fire Prevention ← Billabong 1 10,000L

Fire Prevention

Overflow

Creek → Billabong 2 800,000L

Downpipe ← Shed Roof Water

Overflow

Pump

Waterfall

Creek → Stormwater

Fire Prevention

- - - - Functional Water Catchment
- Functional Water Storage
- Aesthetic Water Storage
( ) Functional Waterway
( ) Aesthetic Waterway
⇒ Water Direction

Plant List

Casuarina glauca prostrate form
Indigofera australis
Leucophyta brownii
Lysiosepalum involucratum
Melaleuca incana 'Velvet Cushion'
Myoporum floribundum
Pimelea nivea
Pultenaea pedunculata
Scaevola albida 'Super Clusters'
Xanthorrhoea minor

Water Table

Annual rainfall	734 mm
Roof catchment area	825 m²
Other hard surface area (e.g. paving or concrete)	42 m²
Potential water to be collected off roof per annum	605,550 litres
Driveway catchment area	1000 m²
Potential water to be collected off driveway per annum	approximately 734,000 litres
Tank capacity	100,000 litres
Billabong capacity	810,000 litres
Size of property	10,000 m²
Permeability % of area	91%

The Synergy Garden

Plant List

Acacia aphylla
Conostylis candicans
Dryandra nivea
Eucalyptus caesia
Grevillea 'Moonlight'
Lomandra affinis subsp. *cylindrica* 'Lime Wave'
Myoporum floribundum
Pycnosorus globosus
Rhodanthe anthemoides
Thomasia pygmaea

Water Table

Annual rainfall	**674 mm**
Roof catchment area	**192 m²**
Other hard surface area (e.g. paving or concrete)	**30 m²**
Potential water to be collected off roof per annum	**129,408 litres**
Driveway catchment area	**50 m²**
Potential water to be collected off driveway per annum	**approximately 33,700 litres**
Tank capacity	**35,000 litres**
Billabong capacity	**35,000 litres**
Size of property	**768 m²**
Permeability % of area	**65%**

Water Diagram

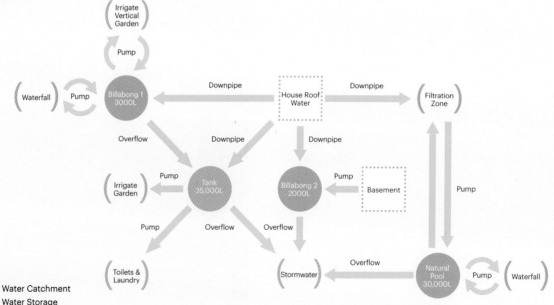

- **Functional Water Catchment**
- **Functional Water Storage**
- **Aesthetic Water Storage**
- ( ) **Functional Waterway**
- ( ) **Aesthetic Waterway**
- ➡ **Water Direction**

The Wetlands

Plant List

Actinotus helianthi

Atriplex cinerea

Austrodanthonia setacea

Brachychiton rupestris

Chrysocephalum semipapposum

Rhodanthe anthemoides

Wahlenbergia stricta

Westringa 'Deep Purple'

Xanthorrhoea johnsonii 'Supergrass'

Xerochrysum bracteatum 'Sundaze' white

Water Table

Annual rainfall	**534 mm**
Roof catchment area	**400 m²**
Other hard surface area (e.g. paving or concrete)	**—**
Potential water to be collected off roof per annum	**213,600 litres**
Driveway catchment area	**1100 m²**
Potential water to be collected off driveway per annum	**approximately 587,400 litres**
Tank capacity	**20,000 litres**
Billabong capacity	**1,345,000 litres**
Size of landscaped area only*	**12,000 m²**
Permeability % of area	**97%**

* Total property area is 5000 acres (2023 hectares)

Water Diagram

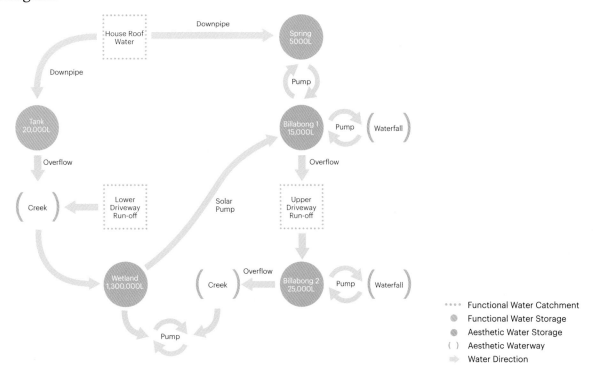

Index

Acknowledgments

There are so many wonderful people who have supported me through this incredible journey. In particular, I would like to thank my beautiful family: my darling wife, Sarah, and our two little boys, William and Angus. Your love, support and guidance over the years have been my driving force and without you, I would never have achieved this. Having children opens your eyes to the world and gives you such a different perspective.

I would like to thank Diana Hill, Gordana Trifunovic, Steve Smedley and Murdoch Books, for believing in my sustainable vision as a landscape designer and providing me with this brilliant opportunity to share my passion with the world. Without their exceptional efforts, this book simply would not exist.

While I can tell you the story of each of these landscapes and describe their tranquil beauty, there is only so much that words can express. Therefore, I am indebted to Claire Takacs and her amazing photographic eye. She has captured the life and soul of every one of these amazing gardens, and her images still blow me away.

I would like to express my gratitude and indebtedness to all those who assisted me during this exciting and rewarding experience. To the whole team over the years at Phillip Johnson Landscapes and, in particular, Vaughn Greenhill for his endless assistance and encouragement, and Brooke Vines Griffin for her enthusiasm, laughter and guidance. I need to thank Marijke McGeehan, Claudia Green and Ray Dubbeld for their horticultural expertise in assisting me with the identification of hundreds of species of plants from twenty years of landscapes. Thank you to Lorelei Vashti and Caitlin Peak for helping to capture my world. I would also like to thank Phil Hill, Jenni Ellard, Michael Schmitt, In Sync, and my dearly departed dog and companion Scruffy, who in his own way, helped us build so many gardens.

Our incredible success at Chelsea in 2013 is something I will never forget, and there are so many people to thank: the team—Fleming's Nurseries and Wes and Paige Fleming, Vaughn Greenhill, Michael Khalil, Leanne Gillies, David Long, Steven Weber, David Pontifex, Mick Conway, Tim Wilkinson, Alistair Tune, Dom Gervigny, Jesse Novotny, Shane Gardner, Josh Schmolzer and Tristain Krepp. Without the dedication and skills of these people, we could never have achieved what we did. You should all be proud of yourselves!

There are also so many people and companies whose belief in our vision culminated in our gold and Best In Show victory. I would like to thank the following for lending their support: everyone at Phillip Johnson Landscapes, Fleming's Nurseries, Trailfinders, Dean Atkinson of Atkinson Pontifex, Lump Sculpture Studio, Dylan Brady and Studio 505, Dave Root and Kelways Plants, Gary Ewing and the team at CED Natural Stone, Membranes Australia, stonemason Callum Gray, Brendan Stemp, Papermill Media, Sarah Sproule and Gun Communications, Eden Gardens, Seasol, Johnson Fine Art, Andrew Kimpton from Made at Yanoit, Victorian Landscape Group, Intergrain, Tankworks, The Green Power Company, Beck & Pollitzer, Angelucci 20th Century, Team Sports Australia, Rolawn, Signex, PhotoSentinal Time Lapse Systems, Rainwell, Gardens At Night, JDM Instant Pumps, Green Lines Gardenware, Apricus Solar Hot Water, Dragonfly Super Skimmer, Franz Kubacek from Hydrobalance, Bulleen Art & Garden, Fultons, Anglo Aquatics, B & I Supplies and Drumhead Sandstone.

I would like to thank the following people for supporting us, believing in us and sending us love and encouragement from across the globe: the partners, wives and families of the entire team, Maria Johnson, Susannah Clarke, Suzanne Litster, Sharon and George Kepper, Barry and Claire Murnane, Bernadette Reeders, Alan and Joan Hart, Allan and Jan Penman, Alan and Sylvia Soderlund, Colin and Val Johnson, Felicity and Peter Williams, Beatrice Moignard, Joanne Diver, Mark Browning, Scott Wynd, Ian Barker, Paul Myers, Roger Greenwood, Kaikai Guo, Nick Dodds, Mick Gibbs, James Maund, Shree Shah, Rock Watson, Mike Jeans, Angus Stewart, Rodger Elliot and Mark Lunghusen, Helen Young and Catherine Stewart, Roger Polson, Mark Tuckey, and Jenni Ellard from Zing Corporate.

I would also like to thank the Honourable Ted Baillieu MLA and the Victorian Government as well as the Honourable Peter Walsh MLA, and the Office of Living Victoria. Having the state of Victoria standing behind us and backing our vision for Chelsea was an absolute honour.

And finally, I owe my thanks to the generosity of the homeowners who were involved in this book, for allowing us to share their stories and their private sanctuaries, and to all our fantastic clients over the last twenty years, I cannot thank you enough for working with us.

Opposite
The Chelsea Garden, from commencement of the build to winning Best in Show.

The Royal Borough of Kensington and Chelsea

CHELSEA EMBANKMENT, S.W.1